# 50

## ✦ AI Prompts

### FOR TEACHERS

Enhancing Your Practice With
Generative Technology

# PAUL J. CANCELLIERI

Solution Tree | Press

*a division of*
Solution Tree

AI outputs featured in the text were generated with the assistance of ChatGPT, Gemini, and Claude.

555 North Morton Street
Bloomington, IN 47404
800.733.6786 (toll free) / 812.336.7700
FAX: 812.336.7790

email: info@SolutionTree.com
SolutionTree.com

Visit **go.SolutionTree.com/technology** to download the free reproducibles in this book.

Printed in the United States of America

FSC
www.fsc.org
MIX
Paper | Supporting
responsible forestry
FSC® C008955

Library of Congress Cataloging-in-Publication Data

Names: Cancellieri, Paul J., author.
Title: Fifty AI prompts for teachers : enhancing your practice with
    generative technology / Paul J. Cancellieri.
Description: Bloomington, IN : Solution Tree Press, [2025] | Includes
    bibliographical references and index. |
Identifiers: LCCN 2024041346 (print) | LCCN 2024041347 (ebook) | ISBN
    9781962188128 (paperback) | ISBN 9781962188135 (ebook)
Subjects: LCSH: Artificial intelligence--Educational applications. |
    Teaching--Aids and devices. | Effective teaching.
Classification: LCC LB1028.43 .C363 2025  (print) | LCC LB1028.43  (ebook)
    | DDC 371.33/463--dc23/eng/20240912
LC record available at https://lccn.loc.gov/2024041346
LC ebook record available at https://lccn.loc.gov/2024041347

**Solution Tree**
Jeffrey C. Jones, CEO
Edmund M. Ackerman, President

**Solution Tree Press**
*President and Publisher:* Douglas M. Rife
*Associate Publishers:* Todd Brakke and Kendra Slayton
*Editorial Director:* Laurel Hecker
*Art Director:* Rian Anderson
*Copy Chief:* Jessi Finn
*Senior Production Editor:* Miranda Addonizio
*Proofreader:* Sarah Ludwig
*Text and Cover Designer:* Abigail Bowen
*Acquisitions Editors:* Carol Collins and Hilary Goff
*Content Development Specialist:* Amy Rubenstein
*Associate Editors:* Sarah Ludwig and Elijah Oates
*Editorial Assistant:* Madison Chartier

# Acknowledgments

While artificial intelligence will play an increasing role as a creative and writing tool for educators, a book like this would never be possible without the support and feedback of talented and thoughtful humans. I am tremendously grateful to Linda Dion, whose creative and collaborative gifts helped me turn the earliest ideas for *Fifty AI Prompts for Teachers* into practical lessons for teachers. Discussions with Linda were the marigold seeds of this project.

The spark that got this book off the ground came from my longtime friend, mentor, and thought partner, William M. Ferriter. Years of conversations and collaborations led to a challenge from Bill in the summer of 2023 to convert ideas into pages. Those ideas were honed by honest feedback from Carrie Horton, Beth Campbell, Justin Osterstrom, Mark Townley, Erica Speaks, and Lauren Miron. Educators improve most when they learn from the best, and I feel lucky to call these fantastic teachers my friends.

I am also grateful to my teaching team and family who both supported me with words and actions throughout the writing process. Without their sacrifice of time and energy, this book would not be possible.

Lastly, I owe a debt of gratitude to the staff at Solution Tree Press, especially President Douglas Rife, who saw the value of this book for educators, and Associate Publisher Todd Brakke, who helped push this work in the right direction. Most of all, I would like to thank my editor, Miranda Addonizio, for guiding this book from rough draft to final work with a kind heart and a willingness to try out so many of the prompts herself and give helpful feedback. It's because of this great team that this book will make a difference for classroom teachers and their students.

Solution Tree Press would like to thank the following reviewers:

Tonya Alexander
English Teacher (NBCT)
Owego Free Academy
Owego, New York

Becca Bouchard
Educator
Calgary, Alberta, Canada

John D. Ewald
Education Consultant
Frederick, Maryland

Rachel Swearengin
Fifth-Grade Teacher
Manchester Park Elementary
Lenexa, Kansas

Visit **go.SolutionTree.com/technology** to download
the free reproducibles in this book.

# Table of Contents

*Reproducibles are in italics.*

## CHAPTER 1

## CHAPTER 2

## CHAPTER 3

## CHAPTER 4

## CHAPTER 5

# About the Author

**Paul J. Cancellieri** is a National Board Certified eighth-grade science teacher at Rolesville Middle School in Rolesville, North Carolina. After spending several years as a science researcher, he began his career as an educator in 2001 and has taught middle school science since then. After ten years in the classroom, Paul spent a sabbatical leading the data literacy program for the North Carolina Center for the Advancement of Teaching before returning to the science classroom in 2014. He has worked at several middle schools in the Greater Raleigh Area, earning Teacher of the Year honors twice. Paul's focus is on grading and assessment, emphasizing best practices for fair and accurate measurement of student mastery.

Paul is a member of the National Science Teachers Association and the North Carolina Science Teachers Association, and he earned the latter's Outstanding Science Teacher of the Year award in 2012. He has also been a member of the International Society for Technology in Education and the North Carolina Technology in Education Society. Paul has presented at conferences for all four organizations, on topics ranging from progressive grading practices to practical ways to use tech tools for learning and assessment. He earned a Kenan Fellowship from the Kenan Fellows Program for Curriculum and Leadership Development in 2011 and has worked every year since with the new fellows to improve their understanding of data and assessment.

Paul earned a master's degree in botany from North Carolina State University and a bachelor's degree in marine science from Long Island University–Southampton.

To learn more about Paul's work, visit his blog *Scripted Spontaneity* (www.scriptedspontaneity .com) or follow @mrscienceteach on X (formerly Twitter), Instagram, Threads, or Bluesky.

To book Paul J. Cancellieri for professional development, contact pd@SolutionTree.com.

# Introduction

Thirty-two minutes before the students of my first class of the day were scheduled to arrive in my eighth-grade science classroom, I had a big problem. A lesson from last year was sitting on my desk. However, exit ticket data from the previous day showed that many of my students didn't have a good grasp on the concepts that they would need for that lesson. I knew that the right thing to do was to postpone the planned lesson and spend some time building the skills and mastery that my students needed. But there just wasn't enough time for me to make those kinds of changes.

It was the fall of 2023, and I had been experimenting with ChatGPT for a few months. Impressed with the quality of the draft text that it could create, I decided to ask the chatbot to help me brainstorm an instructional solution to the situation. Within two minutes, I had five different ideas for remediation lessons that could work with my students. After fifteen more minutes of ChatGPT generation, follow-up prompts, and human editing by me, I had a set of learning stations that would help close my students' learning gaps while also getting them working on the topic of the original lesson I had planned for the day. With just minutes to spare, I had managed to create a better learning experience for my students with the help of artificial intelligence (AI) tools. Moreover, this tool had unlocked my ability to be the better teacher that I wanted to be in that moment.

Artificial intelligence has been an underappreciated part of our lives for years, forming the backbone of voice assistants like Siri and Alexa as well as many recommendation engines for everything from books (Amazon) to movies (Netflix). Since the work of AI occurred mostly behind the scenes, and most people only interacted with it directly by voice, most of us had no idea that a revolution was on the way.

In this introduction, I'll provide a little "tech support" about how AI works as well as discuss the first step you can take on your AI journey—and how this book will support you on that path.

1

## Calling Tech Support: About AI and How It Works

Given that what most people "know" about AI comes from fictional TV shows and movies, it makes sense that many people have misconceptions about what artificial intelligence is and how it works. We think that AI can have emotional responses like Disney's WALL-E, be bent on world domination like Skynet of the *Terminator* movies, or have superhuman abilities to control physical systems like Iron Man's J.A.R.V.I.S. The truth is that modern-day artificial intelligence systems don't function in the same way as human intelligence. Unlike our human brains, which can reason and solve novel problems by applying knowledge to unforeseen situations, current examples of AI lack real-world knowledge and context and work by recognizing algorithms and patterns. Humans can make decisions based on an enormous set of inputs like experiences, emotions, awareness of others, and ethical implications, but AI models are limited to their inputs and training. While AI is currently nowhere near as adaptable as human intelligence, it excels at rule-based tasks, and it is capable of learning from its mistakes (Tegmark, 2018). As educators, we inherently understand this learning process, and we have a unique perspective that can make it easier for us to adopt these tools and appreciate their mechanisms.

Modern AI tools use networks of artificial "neurons" generally modeled after the human brain. Each neuron independently takes input, processes it, and produces an output that is passed on to other neurons. By processing in parallel, these neural networks can perform complex calculations very quickly, analyze their output, adjust, and process again in a feedback loop that mimics human learning (SAS Institute, n.d.). This sort of independent development of artificial intelligence models through iterative feedback is often called *machine learning*. There is some irony in the fact that we might use the result of this machine learning to improve the human learning of our students.

Through machine learning, these neural networks use billions of samples of language and art found on the internet (as well as private data provided by companies and research datasets curated by academics studying AI) to learn to mimic human language and creativity. Beginning in 2018, the companies that developed these networks trained them using the writing of bloggers, authors, social media users, and others, sometimes specially annotated to provide important context. The networks of artificial neurons plotted the relationships between words to show how often they appear near each other in different kinds of writing. These elaborate graphs form the "brains" of the AI models, allowing them to use the neighboring words to predict the next word in a sequence (Lee & Trott, 2023). By repeating this process, the model can generate new text that mimics human writing closely enough to fool most people. Because they were trained with huge quantities of human writing, they were named *large language models* (LLMs).

This was a new and exciting use of artificial intelligence. For the first time, AI could do more than analyze existing data; it could create new content. This category of AI is known as *generative AI*. By applying the same concepts to music and images, LLMs could be trained to make more than just text. The creators of DALL-E, for example, combined words with image pixels to give it the ability to generate new images using simple text as a guide. But access to these tools was limited, and interacting with them still required special software and knowledge of commands. This new category of AI was evolving quickly, and it wouldn't be long before it reached the hands of everyday people.

In the fall of 2022, a cascade of new products was released that included ChatGPT (https://chat.openai.com) and DALL-E 2 (https://openai.com/dall-e-2). These generative AI tools allow people to use natural language commands to create new text, images, and even music using artificial intelligence models—that is, they can use commands in the same way that they could type out messages to a friend. With a simple request, or *prompt*, as these commands are called, ChatGPT could provide paragraphs of text within seconds. Dozens of companies (including Microsoft and Google) joined ChatGPT's parent company OpenAI in building these tools and creating customized versions for different applications (Casey, 2023).

Built to learn, LLMs are also constantly analyzing their own output, and, as the companies behind them provide more computing resources, they are improving the quality of the content that they generate. With their combination of knowledge about nearly every type of instructional content and their ability to create high-quality writing, these AI models have the potential to save you precious time and energy.

## Taking the First Step: How to Get Started Using AI

Any new tool—technological or otherwise—brings with it a learning curve that can intimidate users. Experienced teachers are often (justifiably!) skeptical of whiz-bang new gadgets that promise to revolutionize education but frequently barely move the needle. We have seen so many ideas, strategies, tools, and initiatives fail because they either don't produce results that live up to their hype or aren't financially sustainable. We have seen learning management systems that hold back learning because of their clunky interfaces. We have suffered through the rollout of devices that brought as much distraction as enhancement of learning. Generative AI, however, is different. Rather than promoting a new way to teach and learn, these tools instead augment the professional skills of every teacher.

It's natural to worry that AI will eventually take the place of the educator in each classroom. The public sometimes unconsciously thinks of teaching primarily as the creation and delivery of lessons. The truth, though, is that these lessons are secondary to the work that we do to engage with our students, provide feedback, and foster the human connection from which meaningful learning springs. And so, the true value of these new technological resources is the way they enhance teaching. You decide what your students need to learn, and then ask the AI chatbot to help you brainstorm ways to teach that content. Use your knowledge of your content and your students to decide which ideas are best for your classroom, and then you can ask the AI to help you create the materials that you need. At each stage of the learning cycle that you are designing for your students, you can lean on these artificial intelligence tools for support. In the end, they are only assisting you in maximizing your ability to help your students learn.

Generative AI works in intuitive ways that are surprisingly easy for teachers to learn. Let's take a moment to see how simple they can be by creating some quick content using ChatGPT (or another AI chatbot of your choice). If you have never used one, start by going to https://chat.openai.com and creating an account. It's free to use the basic service, which is all that most teachers will ever need.

Once you have logged into your new account, you'll be presented with a box that invites you to enter a prompt. Let's start with a simple one. I highly recommend actually trying out the prompts in the book as you read.

> **Write a poem in the style of Dr. Seuss that explains how AI works.**

Wait for the output to arrive and read it over. You will likely find that the level of explanation in the poem is appropriate for an adult or maybe for a high school–aged student but not for a younger learner. Your poem might also be a bit on the long side. Let's learn from that first output and rewrite our prompt:

> **Write a poem in the style of Dr. Seuss that explains how AI works. Write the poem at the reading level of a fifth grader and limit it to three stanzas.**

See how adding more detail to our prompt can give us more control over the output? You can also opt to simply add your modifying statements into the chatbot box right after the output appears, like a second prompt. Until you start a new conversation, the AI model will remember your previous prompts and help you home in on what you are trying to create.

Due to the way that LLMs produce novel output, the same prompt can and will produce somewhat different responses with each use. And different LLMs will produce output that shares many similarities—for example, accuracy and common vocabulary—but also display stylistic differences inherent to their training and design. I provided ChatGPT, Gemini, and Claude (the three most widely used general-purpose chatbots as of July 2024) with the following prompt:

> **What is the difference between formative and summative assessment? Explain it in three sentences.**

### ChatGPT:

Formative assessment is conducted during the learning process to monitor student understanding and inform instructional adjustments. It is typically low-stakes and focuses on providing feedback that students can use to improve their learning. Summative assessment, on the other hand, occurs at the end of a unit or course to evaluate student learning outcomes. It is usually high-stakes and aims to measure overall achievement against set standards or learning goals.

### Gemini:

Formative assessment checks in on learning throughout a course. It's like taking a temperature to see how well students are understanding the material. This feedback helps both teachers adjust their teaching and students improve their learning. Summative assessment, on the other hand, evaluates learning at the end, like a final exam. It measures what students have ultimately learned.

### Claude:

Formative assessment occurs throughout the learning process and provides ongoing feedback to improve teaching and learning. Summative assessment, on the other hand, evaluates student learning at the end of an instructional unit or course. While formative assessment aims to identify areas for improvement and guide instruction, summative assessment measures overall achievement and often results in a final grade or score.

As you can see, the models all provide very similar responses, albeit with slightly different tones or word choices (and some exceeding the requested output length to fully answer the question). Each model is also available in both free and premium (paid) versions that differ in some of their features. For example, the most advanced version of ChatGPT and of Claude are both available to free users but for a limited number of daily requests. Gemini (as of July 2024) reserves its most powerful model for premium users, and both Gemini and ChatGPT include image generation in their paid plans. I recommend trying out the free version of all three with identical prompts to see the differences for yourself, and then choose the model that gives you the output you like the most.

Now you can see how simple it is to compose a prompt and get output from an AI chatbot. With just a few words of natural language, you can get the generative AI model to produce some good-quality writing. Next, let's discuss some of the shortcomings that you need to be aware of. AI may eventually take over the world, but right now it needs us to check its work.

- **Beware of hallucinations:** *Hallucinations* is the term that AI scientists use to describe the way these models can sometimes produce statements that are simply not true (Keary, 2023). This problem results from the way that each word is chosen based on its statistical likelihood of being the best choice. The bot can't see the context and doesn't have deep knowledge of the world, just a huge collection of writing to look at. This is why it is so important to fact-check what the AI generates. Sometimes, hallucinations are convincing for someone who doesn't know a lot about a topic. For example, a request I made to ChatGPT for recommended research articles about grading and assessment resulted in four real articles and one fictional one. More advanced models and more detailed prompts usually result in less of this false output.

- **Don't count on breaking news:** The collection of data that an LLM is trained on (often called the *corpus*) is not infinite and is usually carefully selected and annotated to be most useful for the neural network to analyze. Many of the newer models can perform internet searches and may therefore include current events, but this is a weak spot for many of them. Recent news may be less accurate or unavailable, so be careful.

- **It doesn't know everything, but you can teach it:** Some proprietary information and highly specific details—such as the learning standards of most school districts—are not included in the corpus that most models train on. Neither are data that are not located in publicly accessible online databases. But fear not! You can always copy and paste this type of information into a conversation with a chatbot, and it will be capable of incorporating it into its responses.

- **Be careful what you feed it:** After launch, most generative AI models continue to train by reading and processing user prompts and feedback about their output. They use both their output and your prompts as fodder for their continued development in perpetuity. This means that unless you are using a tool that is specifically designed to protect the privacy of your students, you should never upload any private student data or identifying information. Many schools and districts are working on guidance in this area, so be sure to check with yours.

With these caveats in mind, the best general advice for using generative AI chatbots is to try lots of different prompts and variations. One easy shortcut is to prime the chatbot with a clear description of the perspective that you want it to take in helping you. This most commonly takes the form of starting your prompt with a statement of the role that you want it to mimic:

> **You are an experienced elementary school teacher who knows the best way to teach any topic and engage students.**

Or, you can try something like this:

> **You are an expert historian who understands U.S. history very well and is skilled at explaining it clearly.**

Just as these tools learn from humans, we can also learn from them, and through these changes, we can generate a better output.

# Using This Book: How to Save Time and Effort With AI

AI, like few other technologies that came before it, has enormous potential to change education. As teachers, we need to embrace this amazing tool and see the value that comes from handing off some tasks to it and focusing on how we use the output that it provides along with our professional expertise. This book guides you to begin getting the benefit of AI support in your practice. While I hope that the format of this book is largely intuitive, there are some details that will help you make the most of your time reading it.

The chapters in this book are aligned with the steps in a typical learning cycle as defined first by David Kolb (2015) and later by Mike Bell (2020; Marfilinda, Zaturrahmi, & Indrawati, 2019). While many of the prompts described in each chapter can be used in other ways, I've included them with the learning cycle step where they make the most sense and will be most useful.

- **"Chapter 1: Activating and Engaging"**—I share prompts to help plan new units of instruction, capture students' interests, and activate prior knowledge.

- **"Chapter 2: Teaching New Content"**—The prompts here are designed to maximize the effectiveness of new content you teach in your class.

- **"Chapter 3: Reinforcing and Reviewing"**—These prompts help you ensure that students master new content through practice.

- **"Chapter 4: Assessing Student Mastery"**—A critical part of the learning process is determining what students have mastered. The prompts in this chapter provide ways to create authentic and effective assessments.

- **"Chapter 5: Reteaching and Extension"**—Before we move on to new topics, it is critical that we provide extra help for those who haven't mastered the content while also pushing advanced students to deeper learning. These prompts can be useful for both purposes.

Within each chapter, I share ten chatbot prompts (along with variations and alternative ideas) that you can use (and modify for further use) in any chatbot. While chatbots do respond to natural language, choosing just the right words can take some practice and some back-and-forth with the model. The prompts you find in this book will save you time and help you start to integrate more research-proven practices into your classroom.

I explain why I've included each prompt, including the reasons that they demonstrate good quality instruction. I also provide sample output from ChatGPT (using the GPT-4 model) as an example of what may be produced by an LLM in response to the prompt. Keep in mind that your results will almost definitely vary from the sample, even if you use the same tool, due to the nature of generative AI. As I mentioned earlier, different models will yield slightly different results, as will the more advanced paid versions of each model. As these models continue to iterate rapidly, you will find that the current premium models eventually become available for free. If you value the highest quality chatbot output, though, it makes sense to subscribe to the premium version of the model that you prefer.

The sample output this book uses in its examples has been lightly edited for style and to give it a consistent look, but in general, what you see is the output I actually received from ChatGPT. The sample output from each prompt is followed by a section called Change It Up, in which I share some simple ways to change the prompt to get content that is more suited to specific goals. These are just a small selection of suggestions, but remember that any of the prompts are endlessly customizable to your content topics, grade level, timeframe, materials, and much more. If your AI gives you an idea or a piece of content that doesn't look like it will work for your situation, ask the bot to change it. If you find yourself wondering what the output might look like from one of these modified prompts, why not pause, open a web browser window on your smartphone or computer, and test them out yourself? You may find yourself going down a fun and productive rabbit hole as you try out some variations and look at the generated output.

Finally, each prompt includes a section that I call Try It Yourself, where I challenge you to put the prompt to use and reflect on how it works for you. While it may be tempting to skip these sections, you'll find them really useful for identifying the prompts that are most effective in your workflow and capturing how you have successfully modified them. Whether you write down your reflections in the provided area or keep notes somewhere else, I strongly recommend keeping track of the prompts that you use and how you use them in a searchable format, such as in a Google Doc or Microsoft OneNote file. Then, you can simply copy and paste the prompts that have worked for you in the past, providing a springboard for honing these techniques. It's the best way to ensure that AI remains a useful teacher's assistant to you in the future.

While this book can be helpful to individual teachers, it will have the biggest impact when teaching teams use it to make their practice more efficient. When groups of educators work together to identify high-impact strategies and materials, student learning is enhanced greatly. To this end, each chapter includes specific advice for teams looking to incorporate AI into their work together. Additionally, each chapter ends with a set of reflection questions that you can copy or download and share to help stimulate your thinking and team discussions.

Finally, the chapters in this book do well standing alone for those who want to focus on a single part of a learning cycle. However, taking the chapters together in order will allow you to see the many opportunities that exist for these tools to make your job easier at every step of the planning and teaching process. You may find that a prompt that I think works best in one place would be more helpful to you in another. Don't be reluctant to experiment with these prompts—changing them, improving them, and sharing them—as you find ways for artificial intelligence to support you in your teaching.

# CHAPTER 1

# Activating and Engaging

I can clearly remember the look on my student Natasha's face when she realized that she had only answered one question correctly on a twenty-question preassessment about infectious diseases in my eighth-grade science class. She panicked and asked if there was a retest. I responded, "No, Tash, but that's not the point. Did the pretest remind you of anything that you've learned before about viruses?"

She thought about it for a moment, and then her expression changed. "Yeah. I guess. But how was I supposed to know all those things?" she asked. "You weren't," I explained, "but you will understand them much better by the time we finish this unit. The point of the pretest was to dust off the ideas that you already have in your head and get you ready to add some new ones."

Since the constructivist theory was first proposed by Jean Piaget in the early 20th century (Bodner, 1986), educators have known that when we help students connect what they are currently studying with what they have learned in the past, we greatly amplify the power of new lessons (Driscoll, 2000). Activating prior knowledge can have the following benefits (Ambrose, Bridges, DiPietro, Lovett, & Norman, 2010).

- Serve as a bridge that helps students better understand and assimilate new knowledge.

- Motivate students to feel more confident about their ability to learn and become more familiar with the new material.

- Enhance students' ability to recall new information by connecting it to existing memory structures in the brain.

- Lead to a deeper understanding of complex topics as the brain forges connections between them and recognizes patterns.

- Make learning more personal for students by connecting new ideas with those already a part of their own memories, tied to their experiences in and out of the classroom.

- Allow educators to customize learning by observing the mastery level of each student and planning appropriate lessons to move each of them along the road to better understanding of the course content.

For these reasons, effective teachers need to make time at the start of a new learning cycle to remind students of what they have learned in earlier grades and courses. By measuring their prior knowledge about a topic, we reinforce the idea that learning is a continuous process of building on an existing foundation. This is critical to effective instruction, but doing it well requires the preparation of many activities and documents. We need preassessments that include items from previous related courses. We need text and imagery that promote the recall of prior learning. We need collaborative activities that allow those with different levels of prior knowledge to learn from each other. These resources take time and energy to create, and that can be daunting for novice teachers and those who are teaching courses or grade levels for the first time.

And that's where AI tools can help. In this chapter, you will learn about ten different prompts that can be used to generate high-interest lessons and activities customized to meet the needs of your classroom and your students.

## Lighting the Spark: Brainstorm Activities for New Content

The first challenge I face in my classroom each period of each day is to get my students engaged in learning. If students are not paying attention to your lessons, they are unlikely to learn much from them. Frequently, the biggest hurdle is the time and energy it takes to brainstorm ideas for high-interest activities that capture your students' imaginations and get them excited for what's to come. Whether you're teaching something for the first time or the one hundred and first time, it may not be obvious how to make it appealing to your students. Let's look at a prompt that can get us there:

> ✦✦ **Give me five ideas for activities to get elementary school students excited to learn about verbs.**

### Sample Output

Absolutely! Here are five activity ideas to make learning about verbs engaging for elementary school students.

1. **Verb Charades:** Write various verbs on index cards. Students take turns drawing a card and acting out the verb without using words. The rest of the class guesses the verb being portrayed.

2. **Verb Tense Timeline:** Using a long piece of craft paper, create a timeline with Past, Present, and Future sections. Provide students with verb cards and have them place or pin the verb under the appropriate tense.

3. **Verb Song:** Create a catchy song or rap about verbs. Sing it as a class and use actions to represent some common verbs. This could be built upon throughout the unit, adding new verses or actions.

4. **Verb Storytelling:** Students sit in a circle. The first student starts a story with one sentence, emphasizing a verb. The next student continues the story, adding another sentence with a different verb. The story grows as each student contributes, focusing on verb usage.

5. **"Freeze Dance" Verb Edition:** Play music and let the students dance. When the music stops, shout out a verb. Students must freeze in a pose that depicts that verb.

Remember, the key is to make the activities interactive and fun. By doing so, students will have a more positive and memorable experience learning about verbs.

See how these represent a nice variety of ideas? Some of these will require significantly more preparation than others—you aren't going to be writing a catchy song right before class starts—but others could be easily implemented with little prep. The freeze dance and verb storytelling ideas are just the kind of activity that I feel like I could jump right into. They fit my personal teaching style and the existing culture in my classroom well.

If you're more inclined to use manipulatives in your class, the verb charades and verb tense timeline look interesting. If the results don't offer enough variety or you just want more ideas, you can always increase the number you ask for in your prompt. Don't forget (as you'll see with later prompts in this chapter) that the same generative AI tool that gave you this list of ideas can also help you create content for any one of them.

## Change It Up

To make this prompt better suit your needs, try adding modifiers about the specific skill in which you want to spark interest. For example, you might want to focus on the skill of verb tense. Then, your prompt might look like this:

> ✦ **Give me five ideas for activities to get elementary school students excited to learn about how verbs change depending on tense.**

This provides some ideas that include the following.

### Sample Output

**Verb Memory Game:** Pairing game with cards having verbs in base form and their corresponding past or future forms.

**Interactive Verb Wall:** A wall display with movable verbs allows students to change verbs to different tenses.

Or if you have specific types of activities in mind, adjust your prompt like one of these:

> ✦ Give me five ideas for activities that do not require computers to get elementary school students excited to learn about verbs.

> ✦ Give me five ideas for activities that take place outside to get elementary school students excited to learn about verbs.

> ✦ Give me five ideas for activities that must be completed in student groups to get elementary school students excited to learn about verbs.

And, of course, don't forget that you can be as precise as you need to be about the grade level that you are working with.

## Try It Yourself

Now it's time for you to go to your chatbot of choice and try out one of these types of prompts. Use the following space to record the helpful and not-so-helpful bits of output that you received. How would you change your prompt in the future?

---------------------------------------------------------------------------------

---------------------------------------------------------------------------------

---------------------------------------------------------------------------------

---------------------------------------------------------------------------------

---------------------------------------------------------------------------------

---------------------------------------------------------------------------------

---------------------------------------------------------------------------------

---------------------------------------------------------------------------------

---------------------------------------------------------------------------------

---------------------------------------------------------------------------------

# Looking for a Way In: Find the Most Engaging Topic Within a Larger One

Sometimes, we find ourselves teaching a topic that we don't know as well. Maybe we're teaching a new subject or grade level, or maybe we just are not as familiar with the ins and outs of a concept. It can be difficult to know which element of a topic would make a good choice for a high-interest kickoff. We might need help balancing student interest and relevance to the curriculum standards. This is a great task to hand off to the chatbot by asking it to help us rank the topics within a unit by how interesting our students are likely to find them:

> ✦✦ **Rank the topics in Greek mythology by student interest level in each one.**

### Sample Output

It's essential to remember that interest in different topics can vary greatly depending on the individual student, their background, and their personal preferences. However, I can try to list some common topics in Greek mythology that often garner interest, based on the general appeal and frequency in literature and media.

1. **Gods and Goddesses:** Students often show interest in learning about the Olympian gods and goddesses like Zeus, Hera, Athena, Apollo, and others. Their powers, relationships, and stories are rich and diverse.

2. **Heroes and Heroic Myths:** Myths about heroes like Hercules, Perseus, Theseus, and Achilles are popular because of their exciting adventures, challenges, and the moral lessons often included in their stories.

3. **Mythical Creatures:** Creatures like the Cyclopes, Centaurs, Sirens, and Medusa are fascinating due to their unique characteristics and the thrilling stories associated with them.

4. **Epic Poems and Stories:** Epic tales like Homer's *Iliad* and *Odyssey* captivate students because of their narrative depth, complex characters, and the epic journeys and battles they describe.

5. **Creation Myths and Cosmogony:** The origin stories of the world, gods, and humanity provide insights into ancient Greek beliefs and values and are often compared with other cultures' creation myths.

Again, interest can be highly subjective, and educators should try to gauge their particular students' interests and cater to those while providing a broad overview of the significant aspects of Greek mythology.

Again, we get a nice list of ideas that we can use to choose the direction in which we might want to go for an attention-grabbing activity at the start of a new unit of instruction. I think it's awesome that the chatbot cautions me about the subjectivity of student preferences in the output from this prompt. We know from the work of educator and author Carol Ann Tomlinson (2017; Tomlinson et al., 2003) and others that this type of differentiation is critical to reaching every student. As these models become more advanced, you can expect to receive even more of this nuanced approach to using the content generated by these tools.

So, how do we modify this one?

## Change It Up

If you're looking for rankings of specific topics about a standard, try pasting the standard into your prompt like this:

> Rank the topics related to this standard—Explain the significance of Greek mythology to the everyday life of people in the region and how Greek literature continues to permeate our literature and language today, drawing from Greek mythology and epics, such as Homer's *Iliad* and *Odyssey*, and from *Aesop's Fables* [WH6.4.4; California Department of Education, 2000]—by student interest level in each one.

Or, list the subtopics that we already know are part of a unit and ask the bot to rank them by interest level:

> Rank the topics in chemistry (elements, compounds, and mixtures; atomic structure; the periodic table; chemical reactions) by student interest level in each one.

## Try It Yourself

Write your own Looking for a Way In prompt and take some notes in the following space about how well it worked.

---------------------------------------------------------------------

---------------------------------------------------------------------

---------------------------------------------------------------------

---------------------------------------------------------------------

---------------------------------------------------------------------

---------------------------------------------------------------------

# Understanding the Flow: Visualize the Learning Sequence

To better activate prior learning, and to recognize where students have gaps in their mastery of earlier concepts (see Minding the Gaps, page 20), we need a solid understanding of the vertical sequence of learning for a particular topic. For example, as an eighth-grade science teacher, I need to know what my students were expected to learn about chemistry in sixth grade, fourth grade, and earlier.

Understanding the vertical sequence that leads to your content level can make you more capable of judging student readiness and ensuring equitable learning environments (Bergman, Calzada, LaPointe, Lee, & Sullivan, 1998). It also helps make the content more relevant for students as they see how the new learning fits into their existing understanding of a topic.

But this can be a difficult and time-consuming resource to create—unless you let AI do it for you:

> ✦ What is the sequence of learning that Michigan students study about fractions from kindergarten to twelfth grade?

### Sample Output

In Michigan, as well as in many other states across the United States, the sequence of learning about fractions generally follows the guidelines laid out in the Common Core State Standards for Mathematics. Following is a rough outline of the sequence in which students learn about fractions from kindergarten to twelfth grade, though the specific details can vary.

#### Kindergarten to Second Grade

**Kindergarten:** Students begin with the basic concepts of whole numbers and counting.

**First Grade:** Introduction to the concept of parts of a whole.

**Second Grade:** Students begin to work with fractions, understanding that they represent parts of a whole and learning to identify and name simple fractions.

#### Third to Fifth Grade

**Third Grade:** Students develop a more in-depth understanding of fractions, learning to represent them on a number line and beginning to understand equivalent fractions.

**Fourth Grade:** Continued work with equivalent fractions, adding and subtracting fractions with like denominators, and multiplying fractions by whole numbers.

**Fifth Grade:** Students learn to add and subtract fractions with unlike denominators, multiply fractions by fractions, and divide fractions by whole numbers.

### Sixth to Eighth Grade

**Sixth Grade:** Further study of dividing fractions, finding common denominators, and working with mixed numbers.

**Seventh Grade:** Students begin to work with complex fraction operations, including multiplying and dividing fractions and mixed numbers.

**Eighth Grade:** Focus on linear equations and functions, but may also include further study and application of fraction operations in various contexts.

### Ninth to Twelfth Grade

**High School:** The focus shifts more toward advanced mathematical concepts, including algebra, geometry, trigonometry, and calculus. However, a strong understanding of fractions is crucial, as they are integral in these advanced topics.

These stages are generalized and might vary slightly. It's always essential to refer to the specific curriculum adopted by the particular school or district in Michigan to get a detailed understanding of the sequence of fraction learning from kindergarten to twelfth grade.

For more specific and updated information, you should refer to the Michigan Department of Education's standards and curriculum guides or consult directly with the school district in question for their curriculum guidelines.

I love that the output from this prompt even provided resources at the end for finding more information. And I find its description of the progression within a topic to be helpfully concise. Some of these descriptions, though, can be a bit vague—"may also include further study and application of . . ."—and those are places in the sequence where I would ask the chatbot to provide more detail.

This output is also a great example of how our prompts can sometimes be too specific. When I asked about the specific standards of the state of Michigan, the model was forced to generalize. This is why we always need to perform some basic fact-checking before using AI output for important tasks.

## Change It Up

Looking for a more specific sequence? Maybe you want to see how the vertical curriculum can build up to one skill? Try inserting the entire standard into the prompt and asking about what leads up to it:

> What is the sequence of learning from kindergarten to eleventh grade in Michigan that leads to this standard—Understand the concept of a function and use function notation [CCSS.MATH-CONTENT.HSF-IF.A; National Governors Association Center for Best Practices (NGA) & Council of Chief State School Officers (CCSSO), 2010b]?

## Sample Output

In Michigan, the sequence of learning that leads to the standard "Understand the concept of a function and use function notation" [CCSS. MATH-CONTENT.HSF-IF.A] follows a progression from kindergarten through eleventh grade, with each grade building on the concepts and skills learned in the previous years. Here's an overview of this progression.

### Kindergarten to Second Grade

**Kindergarten:** Focus on understanding numbers, counting, and basic addition and subtraction.

**First Grade:** Develop skills in addition and subtraction within 20, understand the basics of place value, and begin exploring measurement and data.

**Second Grade:** Build on place value understanding up to 1000, work with addition and subtraction within 100, and introduce basic concepts of multiplication and division.

### Third to Fifth Grade

**Third Grade:** Introduce multiplication and division within 100, understanding fractions as numbers, and developing concepts of area and perimeter.

**Fourth Grade:** Strengthen understanding of place value for multi-digit numbers, master multiplication and division, and work with fractions, including equivalence and operations.

**Fifth Grade:** Work on operations with multidigit whole numbers and decimals to hundredths, adding and subtracting fractions, and beginning to understand the concept of volume.

### Sixth to Eighth Grade

**Sixth Grade:** Understand ratios and rates, divide fractions, work with multidigit decimals, introduce negative numbers, and begin algebraic thinking.

**Seventh Grade:** Develop proportional reasoning, work with expressions and linear equations, solve problems involving scale drawings and geometric constructions, and introduce probability.

**Eighth Grade:** Work with linear equations, understand functions and using function notation, analyze bivariate data, and understand congruence and similarity in geometry.

### Ninth to Eleventh Grade

**Ninth Grade (Algebra 1):** Deepen understanding of linear equations and inequalities, explore quadratic functions, work with polynomials, and learn about exponential functions.

**Tenth Grade (Geometry):** Focus on geometric transformations, congruence, similarity, right triangle trigonometry, and the application of algebraic concepts to geometry.

**Eleventh Grade (Algebra 2):** Expanding understanding of functions including polynomial, rational, and radical functions, exploring logarithmic and exponential functions, and working with sequences and series.

**Specific Standard in Grade 11**

**High school: Functions—Interpreting Functions (HSF-IF.A):** This standard specifically involves understanding the concept of a function, using function notation, and interpreting functions that arise in applications in terms of the context.

**Breakdown of the Standard (HSF-IF.A)**

1. **Understand the concept of a function and use function notation (HSF-IF.A.1):**

   Recognize that a function assigns to each input exactly one output. The graph of a function is the set of ordered pairs consisting of an input and the corresponding output.

2. **Use function notation, evaluate functions for inputs in their domains, and interpret statements that use function notation in terms of a context (HSF-IF.A.2):**

   Understand and use function notation, e.g., f(x) denotes the output of a function f corresponding to the input x.

   Evaluate functions for specific inputs.

   Interpret statements that use function notation in terms of a given context.

This progression ensures that by the time students reach the standard in eleventh grade, they have a solid foundation in the necessary mathematical concepts and skills built up over the years.

Engagement research has shown that students will invest more time and energy into work that they see as relevant to subsequent levels of schooling (Hulleman & Harackiewicz, 2009). We know this intuitively, and that's why we often point out to our students how our lessons will prepare them for the next year's course. If you are unsure how the current lessons lead into the next, it's easy to adjust the prompt to provide those details:

> ✦ **What is the sequence of learning about statistics that Michigan students will study after sixth grade?**

## Sample Output

I don't have real-time or specific curriculum data for Michigan students or any other location-specific information beyond my last update in 2022. However, I can give you a general sequence of topics that students might typically study in middle school and high school in the context of statistics.

Middle School (Seventh to Eighth Grade)

**Basic Probability:**
Understanding of chance and likelihood
Simple probability calculations
Experiments, outcomes, and events

**Data Analysis:**
Reading and creating tables and graphs
Measures of central tendency (mean, median, mode)
Range and interquartile range

**Simple Surveys and Experiments:**
Designing surveys
Collecting and analyzing data
Making predictions

High School (Ninth–Twelfth Grade)

**Advanced Probability:**
Compound events
Permutations and combinations
Theoretical vs. experimental probability
Sampling and surveys
Financial modeling
Scientific research

The specific sequence and topics can vary depending on the school district, teachers, and available resources. It would be best to check the curriculum of the specific Michigan school district you're interested in for the most accurate and detailed information. You can typically find this information on the school district's website or by contacting the district's office directly.

## Try It Yourself

Pick a topic from your curriculum and ask an AI chatbot to generate the vertical sequence that includes it. How might you use this in your teaching?

# Minding the Gaps: Identify Common Gaps in Student Understanding

No matter what subject you are teaching, there are bound to be students who lack some important skills that they need to be successful in your class. Since the COVID-19 pandemic, this issue is even more widespread. The best way to find these learning gaps, of course, is to use preassessments (check out Finding the Starting Point, page 25). But it's also possible to use artificially intelligent tools to get a preview of the common learning gaps for a particular topic:

> ✦✦ **What are the common learning gaps for students getting ready to study the Revolutionary War in ninth grade?**

### Sample Output

Learning about the Revolutionary War can be a complex task for ninth-grade students due to the multiple facets and perspectives involved in this historical event. Here are some common learning gaps and challenges students might face.

1. **Context and Background:**

   Gap—Lack of understanding of the geopolitical, social, and economic context preceding the war.

   Solution—Integrate comprehensive lessons on colonial America and the European influence.

2. **Complex Causes:**

   Gap—Difficulty in grasping the complex, multifaceted causes of the war, like taxation, representation, and ideological shifts.

   Solution—Use multimedia resources and diverse materials to explain these concepts.

3. **Key Figures and Roles:**

   Gap—Inability to identify key figures and their roles, contributions, and perspectives.

   Solution—Provide biographical studies and analyses to explore these figures in depth.

Each student may face different challenges based on their prior knowledge, skills, and learning styles. Thus, it's essential for educators to be aware of these potential gaps and be prepared with strategies and resources to address them effectively.

Like many sample outputs in this book, this is just an excerpt of the full list it provided. Did you notice that the AI provided solutions and strategies for closing these gaps (without being explicitly asked)? Look for more of this output augmentation as the models gain better context about what the output is likely to be used for. I look through this list for examples of activities that I can use in stations as part of a unit kickoff activity (see Motivating by Rotating, page 36, for station prompt ideas). I can use data from a preassessment (see Finding the Starting Point, page 25) to assign students to the stations that match their gaps. This sort of personalized learning is one of the most powerful strategies available to teachers (Bernacki, Greene, & Lobczowski, 2021).

## Change It Up

Looking for more specificity about the topic or standard that you're teaching? You can make your prompt as specific as you need:

> ✦✦ **What are the common learning gaps for students getting ready to study the Boston Tea Party?**

Or, if you just need an overview (rather than a list of topics), ask the chatbot to limit the size of the output:

> ✦✦ **In two concise paragraphs, what are the common learning gaps for students getting ready to study the Revolutionary War in ninth grade?**

### Sample Output

One common learning gap for ninth-grade students studying the Revolutionary War is a lack of foundational knowledge about the broader historical context in which this war occurred. Students often have a limited understanding of the political, economic, and social climate of the 18th century, both in the American colonies and abroad. They might not be well versed in the relationships between European powers at the time, the colonial governance structure, or the complexities of international trade. Without this background, it can be challenging for students to fully grasp the causes and implications of the Revolutionary War.

Another significant learning gap is related to critical thinking and analytical skills. Ninth graders are still developing the ability to evaluate historical events, sources, and perspectives critically. They might struggle to assess the reliability of different types of sources, analyze varying perspectives, or draw connections between historical events and contemporary issues. Enhancing these skills is crucial for a more profound and nuanced understanding of the Revolutionary War, as it enables students to explore complex questions about power, identity, and revolution, among others. Addressing these learning gaps can be facilitated by incorporating diverse learning materials and instructional strategies that promote analytical thinking and provide a more comprehensive historical context.

## Try It Yourself

Give one of these Minding the Gaps prompts a try. Use the following space to record whether you were surprised by any of the potential learning gaps that the output mentioned.

---

---

---

---

---

---

# Providing a Clear Direction: Craft Student-Friendly Learning Targets

Once you've got an idea of how you'll get started with a topic, it's important to make sure that students know where you're going. In my classroom, this means setting the learning targets for the lessons ahead. For most teachers, the curricular standards are determined by a state or local board of education. Crafted by experts with advanced degrees and with professional educators as their intended audience, these standards can be incredibly difficult for students to understand.

Yet, study after study (and *tons* of personal experience in the classroom) tells us how important it is for students to understand what the end point of a learning cycle is. We know that student engagement and independence are activated by the presence of clearly stated goals (Brophy, 2004; Dweck, 2006; Goodwin & Rouleau, 2022). But the sheer volume of standards makes the task of simplifying their language for students a big lift. The LLMs that power most modern AI chatbots specialize in this sort of task:

> **Rewrite the following standard to make it easily read and understood by a fifth grader.**
>
> **Use combined knowledge of all letter-sound correspondences, syllabication patterns, and morphology (e.g., roots and affixes) to read accurately unfamiliar multisyllabic words in context and out of context [CCSS.ELA-LITERACY.RF.5.3.A; NGA & CCSSO, 2010a]. Include "I can" statements that would prove mastery of the standard.**

## Sample Output

Standard for a Fifth Grader

"I can understand and read big words that I haven't seen before by knowing the sounds letters make, how to break down words into parts, and how smaller parts like prefixes or suffixes change the meanings of words."

"I Can" Statements to Prove Mastery

1. "I can read big words out loud, even if I haven't seen them before."
2. "I can figure out how to pronounce big words by breaking them into smaller parts."
3. "I can remember the sounds that different letter combinations make."
4. "I can understand what a big word means by looking at its smaller parts, like roots or prefixes."
5. "I can show that I understand a new word by using it in a sentence correctly."

I never stop being amazed at how easily the chatbot generates truly student-friendly language at the level I request. I also like that the full standard is broken down and then followed by even more straightforward "I can" learning targets. We know that this type of age-appropriate language is critical for our students to be able to use these statements to set goals and measure learning progress (Nordengren, 2022; Page-Voth & Graham, 1999).

## Change It Up

There are many ways to use this technique with your students. How about taking a standard that they will be learning about years down the road and putting it into language that makes it clear to them why their lessons are important for the future? Like this:

> ✦✦ **Rewrite the following high school standard to make it easily read and understood by a fifth grader:**
>
> **Analyze and evaluate the effectiveness of the structure an author uses in [their] exposition or argument, including whether the structure makes points clear, convincing, and engaging [CCSS.ELA-LITERACY.RI.11–12.5; NGA & CCSSO, 2010a]. Include "I can" statements that would prove mastery of the standard.**

## Sample Output

Standard for a Fifth Grader

Understand how well the author explains their topic or argument, and decide if it's clear, convincing, and interesting.

"I Can" Statements

1. "I can tell if the author did a good job making their point clear."

2. "I can decide if the author's way of explaining is interesting."

3. "I can explain why the author's way of writing is or isn't convincing."

In this simplified version, the standard is broken down into easier language that a fifth grader can understand. The "I can" statements provide clear, actionable items for the student to focus on to show they have learned and understood the concept.

That last paragraph makes it clear that the AI recognizes the purpose of this task. This adds confidence that the output matches our intention, but always closely review the response from the chatbot before using it.

If you teach older students, try rephrasing primary-level standards into the high-level language of the standards. Then, see if your students can pick out the third-grade standard from the ninth-grade one:

> **Rewrite the following elementary school standard to sound like it is written for high school.**
>
> **Describe the relationship between a series of historical events, scientific ideas or concepts, or steps in technical procedures in a text, using language that pertains to time, sequence, and cause/effect [CCSS.ELA-LITERACY.RI.3.3; NGA & CCSSO, 2010a].**

## Try It Yourself

Now, try a version of one of these prompts for yourself. Notice how much easier it is to explain the learning target to your students in this form. How else might you use this ability to rewrite for students?

---------------------------------------------------------------------------------

---------------------------------------------------------------------------------

---------------------------------------------------------------------------------

---------------------------------------------------------------------------------

---------------------------------------------------------------------------------

---------------------------------------------------------------------------------

---------------------------------------------------------------------------------

# Finding the Starting Point: Create Preassessments

While it is important for students to reach a minimum level of mastery in a subject—to earn a passing grade, for example—it is equally important for each student to see themselves as able to make progress. Student engagement is directly tied to students' view of themselves as capable learners (Brown & Ferriter, 2021). One of the best ways for students (and parents and teachers) to see evidence of learning is to have a clear measurement of their content mastery before learning begins. That's the critical role that preassessment plays in the learning cycle.

But building good assessments takes time. And building an additional preassessment can seem unnecessarily cumbersome. We need a tool to make the creation of these preassessments easier, and AI chatbots are great at this:

> **Create a preassessment about target heart rate zones and pre- and postexercise stretching for a sixth-grade student with five multiple-choice questions and an answer key.**

## Sample Output

Preassessment on Target Heart Rate Zones and Pre- and Postexercise Stretching

1. What is the target heart rate zone?

    a. The highest number of heartbeats per minute during exercise

    b. The range of heartbeats per minute that is safe and effective for cardiovascular exercise

    c. The number of heartbeats per minute at rest

    d. The lowest number of heartbeats per minute during exercise

2. Why is it important to stay within your target heart rate zone during exercise?

    a. To ensure you are exercising too hard

    b. To make sure you are exercising at a level that is safe and beneficial for your heart and lungs

    c. To avoid sweating

    d. To reduce muscle soreness

3. What should you do before starting any exercise routine?

    a. Eat a big meal.

    b. Drink soda.

    c. Warm up with light stretching or activity.

    d. Take a nap.

4. Which of the following is a benefit of postexercise stretching?

    a. It increases your heart rate.

    b. It helps to relax muscles and prevent stiffness.

    c. It causes muscle cramps.

    d. It cools down your body too quickly.

5. Which of these is *not* a good example of a pre-exercise warm-up?

    a. Jogging in place

    b. Dynamic stretching (for example, leg swings)

    c. Static stretching (holding a stretch for a long time)

    d. Jumping jacks

**Answer Key:**

1. b. The range of heartbeats per minute that is safe and effective for cardiovascular exercise

2. b. To make sure you are exercising at a level that is safe and beneficial for your heart and lungs

3. c. Warm up with light stretching or activity.

4. b. It helps to relax muscles and prevent stiffness.

5. c. Static stretching (holding a stretch for a long time)

Note that while I kept the example relatively concise, you can ask the chatbot for as many questions as you need to thoroughly test your students' prior knowledge. Think about how providing this answer key to students after they complete the preassessment might start their learning even earlier. Exploring and analyzing assessment data is a proven strategy for maximizing students' feeling of ownership in their work (Andrade, 2019).

## Change It Up

Chatbots can adjust preassessment in lots of ways that we might find useful, such as the format of the question (open-ended, true–false, matching, and so on), and they can even produce rubrics for consistently grading more complex questions:

> Create a two-question preassessment for eighth graders about macronutrients that includes only open-ended questions. Include an answer key and rubric for grading the answers.

And, while paper-and-pencil assessments are a nice start, imagine being able to import an AI-generated preassessment into an online tool that can automatically score the student responses:

> ✦✧  Create a twenty-question multiple-choice preassessment about conjugating verbs in Spanish for ninth graders, in a format that I can import into Kahoot!

## Try It Yourself

See how quickly you can create a pretest by choosing a topic in your class and writing a quick Finding the Starting Point prompt in the style of those in this section. How close is the output to what you would need for your students? How might you modify the prompt to make it even better?

# Creating Mystery: Use Mysterious Stories to Generate Student Interest

Capturing students' interest in a topic, as mentioned earlier (see Lighting the Spark, page 10), is critical to the learning process. This is especially true when starting a new unit of study, and students' lack of knowledge can make it tough to connect them to the new material. Mysteries, though, have a largely universal appeal, hitting a primal part of the human psyche (Brewster & Fager, 2000; Sherrington & Caviglioli, 2020). And a mystery story that involves a new topic of study can be just the ticket for increasing engagement.

Time to put the chatbot to work again:

> Write a mystery story for fourth-grade students that involves photosynthesis.

## Sample Output

**Title:** The Case of the Fading Forest

**Chapter 1:** The Mystery Unfolds

Lily, Max, and Zoe were the best of friends, and they all loved adventure. One bright and sunny day, they decided to explore the dense forest that lay behind their school. They had played there a million times, but this time, something was different. The forest, usually so lush and green, seemed dull and lifeless. The leaves were losing their vibrant green hue.

**Chapter 2:** The Fading Green

As they ventured deeper into the woods, they noticed that the grass, the bushes, and the trees were all losing their green color. The forest was fading. Zoe, the curious one, took out her notebook and began jotting down observations. Max, with his keen eye, started taking pictures with his camera.

**Chapter 3:** The Clue of the Sun

Lily, who loved reading, remembered something about photosynthesis—a process where plants turn sunlight into food and become green. But the sun was shining bright, so why were the plants not green? They decided to seek the help of Mrs. Green, their science teacher.

**Chapter 4:** The Secret Ingredient

Mrs. Green listened to their observation and looked at the pictures Max took. She was intrigued. She explained that for photosynthesis, plants not only needed sunlight but also water and carbon dioxide. The kids wondered if one of these was missing.

**Chapter 5:** The Investigation

They became little detectives. They knew there was plenty of sunlight, and air was all around, but what about water? They started exploring the forest ground and noticed the stream that once flowed jubilantly was now just a trickle.

**Chapter 6:** The Missing Water

Their town had experienced less rain that year, and it was affecting the forest. They decided to talk to the town's mayor about it. The mayor, impressed by their detective work, promised to bring water to the forest.

**Chapter 7:** The Green Returns

The town came together to bring water to the forest. And just like magic, as water seeped into the soil, the green color started returning to the forest. The mystery was solved! Photosynthesis was happening again.

**Chapter 8:** Heroes of the Town

Lily, Max, and Zoe were hailed as the heroes who saved the forest. They realized the power of knowledge and observation. The forest was not just a playground but a living, breathing entity that needed care and attention.

And as they sat amidst the vibrant green, the forest seemed to whisper a thank you. The friends promised to always look out for their silent, leafy companions. They had become not just friends to each other but guardians of the forest.

The end.

P.S. Remember, just like Lily, Max, and Zoe, you too can make a difference by paying attention to nature and taking care of it. Happy adventures!

I like the straightforward simplicity of this story, and I think it's perfect for the intended age group. I also checked the story closely for factual errors, since generated narratives are where AI models more often lose accuracy (Metz, 2023).

## Change It Up

Consider adding to the mystery by leaving it as a cliffhanger. Research shows that unresolved endings engage students even better (Loewenstein, 1994; Sousa, 2024). You can edit the output or—better yet—just ask the AI to write the cliffhanger for you:

> ✦ Write a mystery story for fourth graders about food and energy that ends in a cliffhanger.

In addition to the usual ways to tweak a prompt (for length, topic, grade level, and so on), consider adding elements that will make a connection for your students:

> ✦ Write a mystery story for fourth-grade students that involves photosynthesis and takes place at Rolesville Elementary School.

## Try It Yourself

This is the type of prompt that you will find yourself using outside your classroom the next time you need a fun story to entertain your family or friends. What other story genres might also get your students interested in a new topic? Try it out yourself and put some notes in the following space about the quality of the output.

------------------------------------------------

------------------------------------------------

------------------------------------------------

------------------------------------------------

------------------------------------------------

------------------------------------------------

------------------------------------------------

------------------------------------------------

------------------------------------------------

# Making It Personal: Write Personalized Stories to Capture Student Interest

Another great way to pull students into a new topic is by creating narratives that introduce fresh ideas with familiar characters. I love to use the names of my students, my colleagues, and even our school's principal or custodian in narratives that I build for this purpose. But, naturally, this level of customization can require lots of time. Let's see what the bot can make:

> Write a story that introduces the ideas of theme and tone to seventh-grade students. Be sure to include the following characters: Mr. Cancellieri, Bella, Jonathan, and Mrs. Cooper.

### Sample Output

**Title:** The Enchanted Music Box

Once upon a time, in the small, quaint town of Melodyville, there was a peculiar little shop owned by a gentle and kind old man known as Mr. Cancellieri. The shop was filled with curiosities of all kinds, from glittering gemstones to ancient, dusty books. But of all the treasures in his shop, the most magical of them all was a music box that was said to hold the power to transport anyone who listened to its melody to a world of wonders.

One sunny afternoon, two friends, Bella and Jonathan, ventured into Mr. Cancellieri's shop after school. Bella, with her wide, curious eyes, was always ready for an adventure, while Jonathan, though cautious, could not resist the allure of discovery. They were greeted by the tinkling bell above the door and the soft, welcoming smile of Mr. Cancellieri.

"Welcome, dear children! Feel free to explore the wonders within these walls," he said, his voice a harmonious blend of warmth and wisdom.

As Bella and Jonathan wandered through the aisles, they were drawn to the music box, with its intricate designs and an enigmatic aura that seemed to call out to them. Unbeknownst to them, the music box had not played its melody for years, until Bella's delicate fingers lifted its lid.

As the enchanting tune filled the air, the room around them dissolved, and they found themselves in a magical forest where trees whispered secrets and flowers danced to the rhythm of the wind.

Tone is introduced here, creating a mystical and captivating atmosphere that invites readers into the magical world along with Bella and Jonathan.

They soon realized that each area of the forest was influenced by the different themes of the melodies played by the music box. They met Mrs. Cooper, a graceful and wise old owl who explained the powers of the music box.

"Each melody takes you to a world where the theme is alive; it could be love, friendship, courage, or even sorrow," Mrs. Cooper explained.

As the story unfolds, Bella and Jonathan explore various themes, brought to life through the changing landscapes and creatures they encounter, representing emotions and lessons. For instance, a jubilant melody takes them to a vibrant, joyful world, introducing the theme of happiness. A melancholic tune, on the other hand, unveils a world painted with shades of blue and gray, revealing the theme of sadness.

They also discover that the tone changes with each theme, from lively and uplifting to somber and reflective. The children learn to appreciate the beauty and lessons in each world, understanding that every emotion and experience is valuable.

As they journey through each themed world, Bella and Jonathan's friendship is tested and strengthened, and they gather melodies that reflect their growth and the lessons they've learned.

One day, finding themselves in a world of utter chaos, where the theme of conflict and resolution is intensely alive, they realize the importance of harmony—not just in music but in life and relationships. With the melodies they've gathered, they create a symphony of unity, resolving the chaos and restoring balance.

Returning to Mr. Cancellieri's shop, they realize the music box is not just an object of magic, but a vessel of life's profound lessons. Each tune, with its distinct theme and tone, holds the power to evoke emotions, teach, and inspire.

> In the end, the children understand that theme is the underlying message or lesson in a story, and tone is the way the story feels. Just like in the enchanted worlds they visited, every story they read is imbued with these elements, waiting to transport them to new realms of understanding and imagination.
>
> Their adventure in the magical worlds of themes and tones taught them more than any book or lesson in school ever could. Every time they heard music or read a story, they would be reminded of the enchanted music box and the magical journey that unveiled the wonders of theme and tone.
>
> And as for Mr. Cancellieri's shop, it remained a place of mystery and wonder, where the line between the ordinary and the extraordinary was as thin as the delicate, silvery notes of a magical melody echoing from an enchanted music box.

Reading this story felt to me a lot like reading the final product of a Mad Libs game, except that the facts and details were accurate and supported my curriculum. The story even ends with a clear and explicit explanation of the terms that we asked for. As stated previously, it's extra important to check output like this for mistakes or stylistic choices that may cause your students to become confused about your content. In this example, the story includes the narrative as well as explanatory text about the narrative. You may want to edit the parts that don't fit your goal or would distract your students, using your professional judgment.

## Change It Up

Naturally, you can customize these stories as much as you would like to include as many familiar details as possible. Take it a step further, though, and try incorporating the characters, setting, or plot from a book that students are reading in their English language arts class:

> ✦ Write a story that uses the characters and settings from *A Midsummer Night's Dream* to explain how ecosystems include many interconnected organisms.

Or, get your students involved by asking the AI to leave out the ending of the story and give students a chance to fill it in:

> ✦ Write a story that introduces the differences between the earth's biomes. Be sure to include the following characters: Mr. Cancellieri, Bella, Jonathan, and Mrs. Cooper. Omit the ending of the story.

## Try It Yourself

What's the best story that you can get the chatbot to write using your prompt? What tweaks did you make to your prompt that make the story so compelling and interesting for students? Capture some notes in the following space.

---------------------------------------------------------

---------------------------------------------------------

---------------------------------------------------------

---------------------------------------------------------

---------------------------------------------------------

---------------------------------------------------------

---------------------------------------------------------

---------------------------------------------------------

---------------------------------------------------------

---------------------------------------------------------

## TIPS FOR TEAMS

AI chatbots are not perfect. The source facts and content on which they were trained are time-limited (often only before the year 2021), and the predictive method in which new text is produced can lead to inaccurate statements. The best way to catch and correct these errors is to have multiple experienced educators fact-check AI-generated content. Consider pasting chatbot output into a shared online document (such as Google Workspace or Microsoft 365) and give your team sufficient time to review it and make corrections before any of you use the material with students. Dividing the labor in this way will ensure that you maximize the benefit of the AI tools and the accuracy of the content at the same time.

## Busting Myths: Use Myths to Activate Student Focus

I have found that nothing really motivates a student to closely read a text passage like asking them to find a mistake committed by the author. I take it a step further by identifying several commonly held myths about a new topic, especially when it's something that students have had some classroom exposure to in the past. I reveal that each myth is incorrect and challenge them to explain why. This encourages them to read critically but also to sift through their memories of prior lessons and grab the relevant facts. Let's ask the chatbot to generate those myths for us:

> ✦ **What are three commonly believed myths about the artists of the Renaissance?**

### Sample Output

Certainly! There are several myths about Renaissance artists that have been popularized over the years. Here are three of them.

1. **They Were Solely Inspired by Antiquity:**

   Myth—Renaissance artists were only inspired by classical antiquity and sought to revive the ancient Greek and Roman styles.

   Reality—While the revival of classical ideas was a significant influence, these artists were also inspired by their contemporaries, religion, and various other sources. They melded different influences to create something new and innovative.

2. **Artists Were Independent Geniuses:**

   Myth—Artists like Leonardo da Vinci, Michelangelo, and Raphael worked alone and were the sole creators of their masterpieces.

   Reality—Many of these artists had workshops with apprentices and assistants who contributed to the artworks. Art was often a collaborative effort.

3. **Women Were Not Artists:**

   Myth—There were no women artists during the Renaissance, or they played a negligible role in the art world.

   Reality—Women artists existed and contributed to the Renaissance, but their work was often undervalued or attributed to men. Artists like Artemisia Gentileschi and Sofonisba Anguissola were notable exceptions.

Remember, the Renaissance was a complex period with a diverse array of artists, styles, and influences. While these myths can offer a simplified view of the era, the reality is much richer and more intricate.

These examples are so detailed that I will have plenty of information to create a mythbusting activity. My next step would be to create a student activity in which they would identify (and attempt to correct) the myths. We know that this sort of analysis is a very effective learning tool (Kaiser, 2019; Moss & Brookhart, 2012), especially when it allows students to confront their own misconceptions in a low-stakes way.

## Change It Up

Do you already have a similar worksheet and just want to change the content? Most AI chatbots are sophisticated enough to generate content in specific formats. Try asking for the myths to be composed in a way that can just be pasted into a word processor to make your student worksheet (this example uses a stand-in link to show how you can link to content in your prompts):

> ✦ Rewrite this worksheet for eleventh graders, replacing the myths about metabolism with myths about Hinduism: www.samplewebsite.org/metabolism_mythbusters.pdf

Or, instead of providing a link to a PDF version of the handout that you've used before, you can also just copy and paste the text of the document into the prompt:

> ✦ Rewrite this worksheet for eleventh graders, replacing the myths about metabolism with myths about Hinduism:
>
> Name: _____    Period: _____
>
> Molecular Biology and Energy Myths
>
> For each common misconception about nutrition, metabolism, exercise, photosynthesis, and cellular respiration, try to guess what's wrong and correct it.
>
> Myth: What's wrong about this statement?
>
> Metabolism is just how quickly your body burns calories.
>
> People can't control their metabolism. It's just the way it is.
>
> Skipping meals or fasting is a great way to lose weight.
>
> Lipids (fats) in your diet are bad, and they make you gain weight.
>
> Plants do photosynthesis, and animals do cellular respiration.

Another option is to play a version of the old icebreaker game, two truths and a lie, by asking the chatbot for a mixture of myths and accurate statements. Challenge students to identify the myths and correct them:

> ✦ What are three commonly believed myths about the artists of the Renaissance and two facts about them?

## Try It Yourself

Try out one of these prompts (or a variation) and write some notes in the following space about how you might use these with your students.

-----

-----

-----

-----

-----

-----

-----

-----

-----

# Motivating by Rotating: Create Learning Stations

*Stations* (or *centers*, as they are often called in primary grades) are a great way to give students a wide variety of short learning experiences in one unified thematic lesson. They are proven to be highly effective ways to teach many subjects (Tucker, 2021), including mathematics (Akinoso, Agoro, & Alabi, 2020). Well-designed stations can be a fun way to engage students while connecting their existing knowledge base with new academic content. Rotating students through self-paced activities also frees up the teacher to focus on classroom management and supporting the needs of individual students.

Naturally, however, creating a set of stations is a complicated and involved process that includes brainstorming the activities, creating the written materials and instructions, and setting the stations up. AI models are great at generating ideas for stations and can even make the student handouts, instruction pages, and other written components. By using a chatbot to help create these fun activities, teachers can ensure that this proven strategy is employed more often in their classroom:

> ✦ ✦ **Create a set of three learning stations at which third-grade**
> ✦ **students can get excited to learn about geography. They should**
> **also activate prior knowledge.**

## Sample Output

Certainly! Here are three engaging learning stations tailored for third-grade students to explore geography, incorporating elements that activate their prior knowledge.

**Station 1:** Map Coloring Station

Activity

**Materials:** Paper maps and coloring materials

**Task:** Students color countries and states, label them, and draw known landmarks.

**Prior Knowledge Activation:** Discuss known places and landmarks as students work.

**Station 2:** Clay Landforms

Activity

**Materials:** Clay or playdough

**Task:** Students create mini landforms like mountains, rivers, and so on.

**Prior Knowledge Activation:** Students discuss the characteristics and examples of each landform they create.

**Station 3:** Picture World Tour

Activity

**Materials:** Printed photos of world landmarks, paper, and pencils

**Task:** Students write or draw stories about each landmark.

**Prior Knowledge Activation:** Students recall what they know about each place or landmark.

Reflection and Sharing

After completing all stations, students can present their creations or findings to the class.

A world map can be displayed where students place markers on the countries and cultures they've explored.

Each station uses readily available or easily accessible materials, making it easy for teachers to set up. The activities are simplified yet still interactive and educational, sparking students' interest in geography while activating prior knowledge.

As we have seen before in this chapter, the AI assistant anticipates the information that I would need to set up these stations, including the materials and a description of how prior knowledge is activated. I can look for which station ideas are practical for my learning space and my available resources and ask the chatbot to generate more ideas if needed.

## Change It Up

You can modify this prompt in simple ways to have more control over the stations, including the number of stations and modality:

> ✦ Create a set of five learning stations at which third-grade students can get excited to learn about geography. They should also activate prior knowledge and involve the creation of a digital product.

Or, restrict the stations to specific supplies or technology:

> ✦ Create a set of five learning stations at which third-grade students can get excited to learn about geography. They should also activate prior knowledge. The stations need to use only pencil and paper.

## Try It Yourself

As I discussed previously, many teachers avoid using stations because of the amount of effort needed to make them engaging and impactful to students. Consider a unit or lesson you teach that might benefit from a station-rotation kickoff that you can now create more reasonably with the help of AI. Describe it in the following space.

--------------------------------------------------------------------

--------------------------------------------------------------------

--------------------------------------------------------------------

--------------------------------------------------------------------

--------------------------------------------------------------------

--------------------------------------------------------------------

--------------------------------------------------------------------

--------------------------------------------------------------------

--------------------------------------------------------------------

--------------------------------------------------------------------

## Chapter Reflection

Before meaningful learning of new content can take place, students need to be readied with a combination of activities that provide cognitive connections to existing knowledge. These activities include those that engage students in identifying and activating what they have already learned as well as those that pique their interest in the new topics. This combination ensures that students' minds will have the opportunity to create schema around the new information and understand it more completely.

Teachers have used numerous strategies over the years to make this happen. From hands-on demonstrations to student-paced explorations, we spend countless hours building lessons that make the rest of the learning cycle possible. As you have seen in this chapter, however, chatbots built on AI have the capacity to help teachers brainstorm new ideas and produce the supporting materials to bring these types of lessons to life.

In this chapter, we explored prompts that help plan a new unit (Lighting the Spark, Looking for a Way In, Understanding the Flow, and Minding the Gaps) by giving teachers the information that they need to make important big-picture decisions. We looked at examples of prompts to measure where students are (Finding the Starting Point) and where they need to be going (Providing a Clear Direction). Finally, we used AI to build materials and tasks that would make sure students were ready to learn (Creating Mystery, Making It Personal, Busting Myths, and Motivating by Rotating).

Next, we will discover how artificial intelligence can help teachers create lessons that teach new content.

# Chapter 1 Questions for Discussion

Which prompt produced output that you found most surprising? In what way?

Which prompt did you find the least compelling? In what way would you modify it to make it more useful to you and your students?

What is an engagement or activation strategy that you use that wasn't included in this chapter? How might an AI prompt help you create learning content for it?

# CHAPTER 2

# Teaching New Content

There was a one-way nature to the way that learning happened when I was a middle school student in the 1980s. For centuries, most classrooms placed the teacher at the front of the room to act as gatekeeper for the knowledge that every student was expected to receive and store in their memory. Students were expected to quietly listen or read to absorb the necessary lessons, occasionally practicing them and eventually regurgitating them on a test (Tyack, 1974).

As the internet made knowledge available to anyone with access, and smartphones made that access more readily available, this learning model became obsolete. And in resource-limited communities where internet access is not as widespread, classrooms become oases where access to the internet is nearly universal thanks to government programs like E-Rate (Federal Communications Commission, 2024). Teachers and textbooks no longer needed to be the sources of information, which unshackled educators from the front of the classroom and allowed them to move about the space helping individual students. Our focus could now shift to facilitating learning for each student through dozens of tiny interactions that clarified the lesson in front of them or corrected a misconception that they were too embarrassed to share in front of the whole class.

The idea of student-driven instruction has been around since the open classroom revolution of the second half of the 20th century (Cuban, 2004), but until the COVID-19 remote learning period, its adoption was slow. In the time since, I have witnessed many teachers evolving their lessons to include problem-based learning, authentic assessments such as document-based questions, flipped or blended learning, and other learner-centered techniques. It's exciting to see so many more students getting the opportunity to develop independence while they learn by doing.

Naturally, this transition forces teachers to rethink the materials that they have been using. Sometimes, direct instruction is the ideal way to teach a concept, but other ideas are better served by students researching a group project or analyzing real data. Creating the right mix of lessons for your students takes time and effort, and there are many ways that AI can help. In this chapter, you will explore ten prompts to create a wide variety of lessons and materials that you can use to help students learn new information.

## Avoiding Reinventing the Wheel: Modify Existing Documents and Materials

Sometimes the most efficient use of your time is to use what you already have, updating or adding to existing lessons that have already worked for you and your students in the past. Maybe the references to events and people are no longer current. Or, the lesson flopped the last time you taught it. Let's try modifying an existing document with help from an AI chatbot. First, review the original handout that I used for this example (see figure 2.1).

Handout contents can be included in the prompt by copying and pasting, linking, or uploading the document file directly using the chatbot's interface. Let's try it with the example from figure 2.1:

> ✦ Rewrite this handout to make it more interesting to fifth-grade
> students: [Pasted document contents]

### Sample Output

Here's a rewritten version of the handout, making it more engaging and relatable for fifth-grade students:

---

### 🚀 **Mission:** Energy Adventure—A Day as a Middle School Super Agent

#### 🔍 **Secret Briefing:** Powering Up With Food!

Hey Super Agents! Did you know that the energy you get from munching on your favorite snacks and meals is measured in something called calories? It's like fuel for your body's engine! Your mission is to balance the energy you gain from food with the energy you use in your super cool activities.

Calorie Power Sources

**Carbo-Boosters:** 1 gram gives you 4 energy points (calories).

**Fat-Fuel:** 1 gram is a powerhouse with 9 energy points.

**Protein-Power:** 1 gram equals 4 energy points, just like Carbo-Boosters!

💡 **Spy Tip:** Use these secret codes to figure out how much energy you're getting from different foods!

## Introduction to Macronutrients

Macronutrients are nutrients that our bodies need in large amounts to give us energy and keep us healthy. There are three main types of macronutrients.

1. **Carbohydrates:** These are the body's main source of energy. They can be found in foods like bread, pasta, fruits, and vegetables.
2. **Proteins:** These are essential for building and repairing tissues in our body. Foods high in protein include meat, beans, eggs, and nuts.
3. **Lipids (Fats):** These provide long-term energy storage and help protect our organs. Examples of foods high in fats include butter, oils, and avocados.

### Understanding Calories

Calories are a way to measure the amount of energy that food provides. When we eat food, our bodies use the calories for energy to move, think, and grow. Different foods have different amounts of calories.

### Part 1: Fill in the Blanks

1. The three main types of macronutrients are _____, _____, and _____.
2. _____ are nutrients that our body uses for energy and to build cells.
3. _____ provide the most energy per gram compared to other macronutrients.
4. _____ are important for building muscles and repairing tissues.
5. The amount of energy in food is measured in _____.

### Part 2: Matching

Match the macronutrient to its function.

A. Lipids    B. Proteins    C. Carbohydrates

1. _____ Provides quick energy
2. _____ Helps in building and repairing tissues
3. _____ Provides long-term energy and insulation

### Part 3: True or False

_____ Lipids are the main source of energy for our body.
_____ Proteins can be found in meat, beans, and nuts.
_____ Calories are a type of macronutrient.
_____ Carbohydrates include sugars and starches.
_____ All foods have the same amount of calories.

### Part 4: Short Answer

1. Name three foods that are high in carbohydrates.

_____

2. Why are proteins important for our body?

_____

3. How do lipids help our body besides providing energy?

_____

### Part 5: Calorie Counting

Look at the following food items and write down the number of calories.

- An apple (95 calories)
- A slice of bread (70 calories)
- A glass of milk (150 calories)

1. If you eat two apples, how many calories have you consumed? _____
2. If you have a sandwich with two slices of bread and a glass of milk, how many calories have you consumed? _____

*Figure 2.1: Handout example.*

Training Exercise: Food Energy Decoder!

**Example Mission:** If you eat a Super-Sandwich with 46 g of Carbo-Boosters, 24 g of Protein-Power, and 10 g of Fat-Fuel, you get 370 energy points!

**Your Turn:** Decode the energy in a slice of Mega-Lasagna: 32 g Carbo-Boosters, 19 g Fat-Fuel, 27 g Protein-Power. How many energy points?

✹ **Part 1:** Day of a Middle School Super Agent

Operation Instructions

**Your Task:** Track your energy points gained from food and used in activities during a school day. Combine positive (energy gained) and negative (energy used) numbers.

**Your Goal:** Balance your energy! If your points are zero, you're in perfect balance. Positive? You're gaining energy. Negative? You're using more than you're getting.

**Agent Schedule:** Energy Tracking

| Time | Spy Activity | Energy Points |
|------|--------------|---------------|
| 5:30 a.m. | Recharge (Sleep) | –480 points |
| 6:00 a.m. | Prep for Mission (Shower and Dress) | –78 points |
| 6:15 a.m. | Power Breakfast | +793 points |
| . . . | Continue with your day's activities . . . | |

✐ **Mission Log:** Fill in your energy points and calculate your net energy.

**Discussion:** If your energy points are not at zero, think like a Super Agent! What changes would you make to your diet or activities?

🏃 **Part 2:** Exercise Challenge—The Cheeseburger Conundrum

**Quick Poll:** Do you think a three-minute Power Run is enough to zap the energy from a cheeseburger? Yes/No. Why?

**Action Time:** Jog in place for three minutes. Check the cheeseburger's energy points.

**Reflection:** Revisit your answer from part 1. How long do you think it takes to zap those cheeseburger points?

**Super Agent Calculation:** How many points did Emmanuel zap in three minutes? Calculate your mission time to zap the cheeseburger energy.

**Alternative Mission:** What other super activities can zap the cheeseburger energy and how long would it take?

End of Mission! ✹

---

This version introduces a more playful and engaging theme, using terms like *energy points* and *Super Agent* to make the content more relatable and fun for fifth graders. The interactive elements and scenario-based learning encourage active participation and critical thinking.

See how the AI took the original idea and made it more fun and accessible with the addition of emoji and a spy mission theme?

This is a fantastic starting point for making an activity better. I love the inclusion of emoji to capture students' interest as well as make the sections of the worksheet clearer. And by recasting this activity, rather than starting fresh, you can feel confident that it will address the same learning targets as the original. After a little proofreading to check the accuracy of the new text, this would be ready to share with students much faster than if it was a brand-new lesson.

## Change It Up

Now, imagine that you have an activity that requires specific tools or space that you don't have access to. You can modify the prompt to make specific changes to the activity:

> **Rewrite this activity to work with only one classroom computer: [Pasted document text]**

The first output from this prompt suggested that students use their own devices or the classroom computer to complete some of the technology-enhanced activities. In my school, students are not allowed to use their own devices in class, so I rewrote the prompt to get ideas that did not use technology at all. Don't give up if the initial suggestions from the chatbot don't fit your situation; add more details to the prompt and try again.

What if you have a set of sample mathematics problems that include dated pop-culture references (How fast *did* the Concorde fly when it was in use ten years before my students were born?) that need updating to maintain their relevance to your students? Copy and paste them into a prompt that asks for newer ones:

> **Rewrite these word problems to include things popular in 2023:**
>
> In an episode of the popular '90s TV show *Friends*, Joey and Chandler buy a new foosball table. Joey pays 2 times more than Chandler. Together, they pay $150 for the table. Let $x$ represent the amount Chandler pays. Write an equation to find out how much Chandler paid for the foosball table and solve it.
>
> If you're playing *Pac-Man* on your Atari, suppose each ghost, Blinky, Pinky, Inky, and Clyde, gives the same amount of points. Pac-Man starts the level with 1,500 points. If Pac-Man eats 3 ghosts and then finds a fruit worth 100 points, his score becomes 2,200 points. How many points does each ghost provide? Let $g$ represent the points per ghost. The equation to solve is $1500 + 3g + 100 = 2200$.

**Sample Output**

1. In a recent episode of the hit streaming series *Stranger Things*, Mike and Eleven go shopping for a new virtual reality gaming set. Mike contributes 2 times more than Eleven. Together, they spend $300 on the set. Let $x$ represent the amount Eleven contributes. Write an equation to find out how much Eleven paid for the gaming set and solve it.

2. If you're playing *Fortnite* on your latest gaming console, imagine each elimination of an opponent scores the same amount of points. A player starts a match with 2,000 points. If the player achieves 3 eliminations and then completes a mission worth 200 points, their score reaches 3,700 points. How many points does each elimination provide? Let $g$ represent the points per elimination. The equation to solve is $2000 + 3g + 200 = 3700$.

While it's important to double-check the calculations on both examples, they seem to be a great solution to the problem of how to update older texts to include more relevant and engaging references. When the bot makes the word problems, it may change the numbers as well, so consider asking for a new answer key with your output. Keep in mind (as I discussed in the introduction, page 1) that most generative AI models do not have the very latest popular culture data. If you find that it isn't including the references that your students will recognize, you can always insert the references yourself:

> **Rewrite these word problems to include a family of animated talking Australian dogs named Bluey, Bingo, Bandit, and Chilli.**

## Try It Yourself

While these prompt ideas are fresh in your mind, try updating one of your digital documents using a chatbot and record your reflection in the following space. How successful was your attempt? How might you use this strategy this year?

-------------------------------------------------------------------------

-------------------------------------------------------------------------

-------------------------------------------------------------------------

-------------------------------------------------------------------------

-------------------------------------------------------------------------

-------------------------------------------------------------------------

# Explaining It Better: Find the Right Metaphor for Every Concept

Perhaps because I am a science teacher, spending most of my class time trying to help my adolescent students wrap their heads around complex processes and abstract ideas, I love finding just the right metaphor to explain something. There is something about that moment when you see the student make the connection between a familiar idea and the more sophisticated one. It is often a fleeting moment of joy, because what helps one student understand a difficult topic sometimes will not click at all for another one. What if you could generate lots of good analogies and metaphors for a topic? You'd have many more tools in your toolbelt and much more success in your explanations:

> ✦ **Give me five metaphors that can be used to explain compound interest to a sixth grader.**

### Sample Output

Certainly! Here are five metaphors that can help explain the concept of compound interest in a way that a sixth grader can understand.

1. **Snowball Rolling Downhill:** Just like a snowball gets bigger as it rolls down a hill, your money grows larger with compound interest.

2. **Planting a Seed:** Think of compound interest like planting a seed. The initial investment is the seed, and over time, it grows into a large tree.

3. **Baking a Cake:** Your initial investment is like the ingredients of a cake. Over time, with compound interest, it "bakes" into a bigger cake.

4. **Building Blocks:** Each interest payment is like adding another block to a tower. The more blocks you have, the taller your tower becomes.

5. **A Family Tree:** Your initial investment is like the first generation, and the compound interest is like the children and grandchildren that keep adding on.

These metaphors relate to familiar concepts or experiences that can help make the idea of compound interest more understandable for a young student.

I really love how diverse the collection of examples in the sample output is. In an AI-generated list of this length, you'll notice some repetition and overlap, so look over the output carefully to pick out the winners. There is bound to be an idea here that will help any student comprehend this specific mathematics concept. When students connect a classroom concept with an analogy or metaphor, identifying similarities and differences between what they know and understand and what they are being asked to assimilate, they gain up to 45 percent more mastery (Marzano, 2017; Marzano, Pickering, & Pollock, 2001). That's why it's so important that you find and use metaphors to make complex ideas more understandable to students.

## Change It Up

But what if you want your students to play a bigger role in choosing and using the analogies? Maybe you've read education researcher and author Robert J. Marzano's (2017; Marzano et al., 2001) research, and you see that you can get more bang for your instructional buck by making students more active in the process. Later in the learning cycle—when students have some background knowledge of a topic—give them a list of different analogies and have them pick one to use. You can ask them to describe how the analogous system or object is similar and different from the concept that they are exploring in class. And a simple change to our chatbot prompt will get you a list of choices:

> ✦ **What are five analogies that high school students could choose among to connect with the concept of complex numbers?**

### Sample Output

Creating analogies for complex numbers can be a fun and effective way to help high school students grasp this mathematical concept. Here are five analogies that could be useful.

1. **Coordinates on a Map:** Just like you need two coordinates (latitude and longitude) to pinpoint a location on a map, complex numbers use two components (real and imaginary) to define a point on the complex plane.

2. **3-D Movies:** In 3-D movies, two images are combined to create depth perception. Similarly, complex numbers combine real and imaginary parts to add depth to the number system.

3. **Book and Bookmark:** Think of the real part of a complex number as a book (the main story), and the imaginary part as a bookmark (an extra tool). Both are needed for the full reading experience, just as both parts are needed for a complete complex number.

4. **Recipe Ingredients:** A recipe needs a combination of ingredients to make a dish. Similarly, complex numbers require both real and imaginary parts to create a complete number.

5. **Computer Graphics:** Just like computer graphics use $x$ and $y$ coordinates to create images, complex numbers use real and imaginary parts to represent points and create images on the complex plane.

You can also ask for more options and then choose three to five that you would give students. I would also leave out the explanation that the AI provides. You can use what you know about your students and your content to help make those choices. For example, I think my students would connect with the idea of 3-D movies showing more depth by having information for each eye, but they might not understand the computer graphics example because they don't know how computers make images. But you don't need to make the choice for them. By having students choose the analogy and explain its connection, you help them develop critical-thinking skills while preserving a powerful element of choice to motivate them.

## Try It Yourself

Metaphors and analogies are powerful tools for explanation and connection to prior learning. Consider a complex topic in your curriculum that students often struggle to understand and use an AI chatbot to help you choose effective analogies to help them understand it better. What was your favorite AI-generated analogy?

----------------------------------------

----------------------------------------

----------------------------------------

----------------------------------------

----------------------------------------

----------------------------------------

# Leaning Into Literacy: Generate Customized Reading Passages With Supporting Activities

Numerous studies (Anders & Guzzetti, 2005; Heller & Greenleaf, 2007) have demonstrated the need for student literacy as a fundamental building block that eventually leads to better understanding of other topics, like science and history. But providing students with texts that can offer the right topic, reading level, and length can be a real challenge for busy teachers. And that doesn't even include the time it takes to prepare supporting activities like anticipation guides, comprehension questions, and annotation tasks. Many teachers are forced to use less relevant or appropriate passages that just happen to be available, or they simply avoid giving their students reading practice at this stage in the learning cycle. But it doesn't need to be this difficult. Let's put the chatbot to work making your job more feasible:

> ✦✦ **Write a five-paragraph passage that explains CRISPR, written for fifth graders. Include an anticipation guide with five questions.**

### Sample Output

Anticipation Guide for CRISPR (Fifth-Grade Level)

Before reading about CRISPR, think about these questions.

- What do you think CRISPR is? Is it a tool, a machine, or something else?
- Can you guess how scientists might use CRISPR in real life?

- Do you think CRISPR can change the traits of living things? Why or why not?

- Have you heard of genes and DNA? How do you think they relate to CRISPR?

- Do you think CRISPR is something new or has it been around for a long time?

Understanding CRISPR: A Guide for Fifth Graders

**Paragraph 1:** Introduction to CRISPR

Imagine you are an artist with a magic eraser that can change any part of your drawing instantly. In the world of science, there is a tool kind of like this magic eraser, and it's called CRISPR. CRISPR is not a drawing tool but a special method scientists use to change the genes of plants, animals, and even humans. Genes are tiny parts inside every living thing that decide what it looks like and how it behaves.

**Paragraph 2:** What Is CRISPR?

CRISPR stands for Clustered Regularly Interspaced Short Palindromic Repeats. That's a big, complicated name, but you can just remember it as CRISPR. It's a natural system that bacteria use to protect themselves from viruses, kind of like how our bodies fight off a cold. Scientists learned how to use CRISPR to cut DNA at specific spots. DNA is like a recipe book for every living thing, telling it how to grow and what to become.

**Paragraph 3:** How Does CRISPR Work?

Think of DNA as a long string of letters that spell out instructions for how a living thing should look and act. Sometimes, there might be a mistake in these instructions, like a misspelled word. CRISPR can be programmed to find this mistake, cut it out, and replace it with the correct letters. This is like fixing a typo in a sentence to make it right.

**Paragraph 4:** Uses of CRISPR

Scientists use CRISPR for many amazing things. They can make crops grow better, help animals resist diseases, and even try to cure human illnesses. For example, they might change the genes in a plant to make it stronger against bugs or bad weather. In humans, they're researching ways to use CRISPR to fix genes that cause diseases, so people can live healthier lives.

**Paragraph 5:** The Future and Importance of CRISPR

CRISPR is a powerful tool, and like all powerful tools, it must be used carefully. Scientists are still learning about all the ways CRISPR can help and the importance of using it responsibly. As we understand more about it, CRISPR could help us solve some of the biggest problems in medicine, farming, and the environment. It's an exciting area of science that shows how understanding nature can lead to incredible discoveries.

After reading, think about the questions again. How has your understanding of CRISPR changed? Do you see how important it is in science and the potential it has for the future?

Your first task, as always, is to fact-check the content in this reading passage. As I've discussed previously, the chatbot doesn't "know" about CRISPR. Rather, it's using the text that it's been trained on to predict what words would likely come next. So, use your expertise (and perhaps some research, if necessary) to make sure that the explanations are accurate. Lean on curricular materials provided by your school or district, and don't be afraid to ask your school librarian or media literacy teacher for a list of trusted websites to use for verification of details in the output.

Did you notice that the generative AI model placed the anticipation guide at the top of the output, even though I tacked it on to the end of the prompt? It recognized that it would likely be used before the reading. I also appreciate that each paragraph is labeled, although I would remove some of that to make the text flow better and the passage feel more cohesive. Overall, though, I was impressed that it recognized what the purpose and format of an anticipation guide would be. So, how can you use this technique to create even more reading resources?

## Change It Up

Consider all the ways that you can change the content and format of the reading passage itself, whether by reading level or format. You can use this technique to differentiate the passage for various readers in your classroom (struggling readers get a reading passage at their level, while more adept readers get challenged with a more rigorous text about the same content) or to make it easier to build assessments or read aloud in class (numbering the lines or emphasizing important vocabulary words):

> Write a five-paragraph passage that explains CRISPR, written at Lexile level 300. Underline the important vocabulary words.

> Write a five-paragraph passage that explains CRISPR, written for advanced fifth graders. Number the paragraphs along the left-hand side.

Or, think about the other types of supporting activities and resources that might be helpful to have with a reading passage, like a glossary or comprehension questions:

> Write a five-paragraph passage that explains CRISPR, written for fifth graders. Add a glossary of important terms and definitions at the end.

> Write a five-paragraph passage that explains CRISPR, written for fifth graders. Include five multiple-choice comprehension questions and an answer key.

Once you have a passage, remember that AI chatbots treat their prompts as conversations. That means that you can follow up a request with subsequent modifications that will take into account the context of the initial prompt. And when the model fails to give you what you've asked for, use additional requests to fine-tune the output:

> **Now turn this passage into a Cloze activity with the following words removed and the answers provided: DNA, edit, CAS-9, enzyme.**

## Sample Output

Cloze Activity Passage

CRISPR is like a very tiny pair of scissors for genes. Imagine if you had a set of building blocks, and you could change the shape of one block to make your building even cooler. That's what CRISPR does, but with the tiny building blocks inside every living thing, called genes.

First, let's think about what genes are. Every living thing, like plants, animals, and even you, are made up of tiny cells. Inside these cells are genes, which are like instructions that tell the cell what to do. These instructions decide everything about how a living thing looks and acts. If we think of a cell like a tiny factory, genes are the factory's instruction manual. The instruction manual is made of a special code called _____.

Now, here's where CRISPR comes in. Sometimes, there might be a mistake in the genes, like a typo in our instruction manual. This typo can cause problems, like making a plant sick or causing a disease in humans. Scientists use CRISPR to find these mistakes. It's like a detective with a very small magnifying glass, looking for clues in the genes. CRISPR works with a special helper called _____, which is like the scissors that do the cutting.

Once CRISPR finds the mistake, it uses its tiny scissors to cut the gene at that exact spot. Then, scientists can either remove the bad part or replace it with a good part. It's like fixing a typo in a book, so the story makes sense again. This can help cure diseases, improve crops, and even help endangered animals. The process of changing the part of a gene is called _____.

But remember, CRISPR is a powerful tool, and scientists are still learning how to use it safely and wisely. It's important to think about how changing genes might affect the living thing and everything around it. Just like with any tool, it's important to use CRISPR carefully and thoughtfully. The tool that CRISPR uses to cut the DNA is a type of _____.

Answers

1. DNA

2. CAS-9

3. Edit

4. Enzyme

## Try It Yourself

This type of prompt is powerful and versatile. Think of a topic that you are teaching that needs more reading practice and supports for students. Try a few of the prompts from this section and record your results in the following space.

---

---

---

---

---

---

---

# Scripting Your Presentation: Create Outlines for Instructional Slide Decks

Many teachers use interactive slide decks—in Microsoft PowerPoint or Google Slides, for example—as a particularly effective way to share new concepts with students, often through direct instruction. It's easy to create slides that explain necessary background information, describe the history of a topic using a timeline, provide important visual elements like photos or graphs, or lay out a progression of ideas in a linear way. Whether students navigate these resources on their own or you use them as a teacher-paced slideshow, they represent a blank canvas that you can fill with text, images, videos, and links to convey important learning.

But building these slide decks can be very challenging. If you are new to teaching a specific topic, you may not be able to visualize the best flow of slides to explore it. Even if you know a topic well, the time needed to design and build engaging slides is considerable. While a simple web search will uncover lots of examples of AI tools that will attempt to build basic slide decks using your outline, most of these tools are expensive or ineffective (Rudra, 2023). The good news is that text-based generative AI chatbots can help plan out the best way to present information in your slide decks, suggesting text and images that provide the idea flow. Let's give it a try:

> ✦ Help me create a slide deck to explain the different types of adverbs to a sixth grader.

**Sample Output**

Creating an educational slide deck for sixth graders about the different types of adverbs can be both informative and engaging. Here's a suggested structure for your slide deck:

Slide 1: Title Slide

- **Title:** "Exploring the World of Adverbs"
- **Subtitle:** "Understanding How Adverbs Spice Up Our Sentences"
- **Image:** A fun, colorful illustration of various adverbs floating around.

Slide 2: Introduction to Adverbs

- **Title:** "What Is an Adverb?"
- **Content:** Briefly explain what adverbs are and their role in a sentence.
- **Example:** Show a simple sentence and highlight the adverb.
- **Image:** A cartoon character thinking about a sentence with an adverb highlighted.

Slide 3: Types of Adverbs—Manner

- **Title:** "Adverbs of Manner"
- **Content:** Explain adverbs of manner and how they describe the way something is done.
- **Examples:** *quickly, slowly, happily*
- **Activity:** A short exercise asking students to match adverbs of manner to actions.

For the images, it would be effective to use colorful, engaging illustrations that match the content of each slide. This can help maintain the attention of sixth graders and make the learning process more enjoyable.

I have included the first three slides it provided; the original answer gave eleven! Notice that the strength of the AI model is in how it chunks the content into suitable pieces and creates an appropriate sequence to present them. As with so many uses of artificial intelligence in the classroom, this output assists the professional educator in the brainstorming and design process but leaves it to the teacher to decide on the details that will resonate most with their students. In its full answer, the bot provided further content-rich slides, fun facts, a short assessment, and additional resources. I can omit any of these as I build the slide deck and consider the time available and preexisting knowledge of my students. The inclusion of additional resources would be great for using the slide deck as an asynchronous resource that students explore independently.

## Change It Up

How can you modify this type of prompt to adapt the output to other situations? What if you already have a slide deck that you want to improve on? You can upload it (as a PowerPoint file or a PDF) to the chatbot and ask for suggestions to improve it:

> ✦ How would you make this slide deck more interactive and easier for students to understand?

Once you have an instructional slide deck that you want to use with your students, wouldn't it be great if you could give students a handout that guides them through exploring it? Or a quiz to ensure that they understand the critical details in the slide deck? You can upload your slide deck and ask the AI to analyze it and produce these supplemental resources:

> ✦ Analyze the attached slide deck and create a ten-question quiz about it with an answer key.

Remember how the AI gave us descriptions of suggested images for each slide? We can use other generative AI tools to create these images easily. By accessing image-generation AI tools like DALL-E (https://openai.com/dall-e-2) or MidJourney (https://midjourney .com), we can use the text from our sample output as the prompt. In fact, some AI chatbots are beginning to integrate with image-generation tools to make it easier to generate images from natural-language prompts in the same entry box that you would use for generating text. Creating images this way saves the time it would take to find suitable images and can minimize issues navigating copyright.

## Try It Yourself

Now, head over to a chatbot window and give these ideas a try. Don't forget to try uploading existing slide decks to get help making them more interactive. What was your best output? Write about it in the following space.

-----------------------------------------------------------------------------

-----------------------------------------------------------------------------

-----------------------------------------------------------------------------

-----------------------------------------------------------------------------

-----------------------------------------------------------------------------

-----------------------------------------------------------------------------

-----------------------------------------------------------------------------

-----------------------------------------------------------------------------

# Getting Their Hands Dirty: Brainstorm Hands-On Lessons

The value of applied or experiential learning is well known to educators in many fields (Kontra, Lyons, Fischer, & Beilock, 2015). I have found that many teachers wish for ways to make their content more kinesthetic using manipulatives and equipment. While some subjects lend themselves more easily to hands-on learning—science, for example—students need concrete exposure to many topics to fully comprehend them. The challenge is to figure out how best to create these experiences. Here's how we can ask the generative AI for help:

> ✦✦  **What are three hands-on activities that can be used to teach students about working with polynomials for ninth graders?**

### Sample Output

Teaching polynomials to ninth graders can be more engaging and effective with hands-on activities. Here are three activities that can help students better understand and work with polynomials.

1. **Polynomial Puzzles:** Create puzzles where students need to match different polynomial expressions with their simplified forms or factorized forms. For example, one piece of the puzzle could have $2x^2 + 8x$ and students would need to find the matching piece with $2x(x + 4)$. This can be done with physical puzzle pieces or as an interactive online activity.

2. **Graphing Polynomials:** Use graphing software or graphing calculators to help students understand the shapes of polynomial graphs. They can plot different polynomials and observe how changes in the coefficients and powers affect the graph. This visual representation helps in understanding concepts like end behavior, zeroes, and turning points.

3. **Creating Polynomial Art:** Students can create art by designing patterns or pictures on a coordinate grid using polynomial equations. This activity not only encourages creativity but also enhances their understanding of how equations translate into graphical representations.

These activities not only make learning about polynomials more interactive but also help students understand and retain the concepts more effectively.

The variety of activities suggested by the chatbot gives me the flexibility to choose the ones that are most feasible for my classroom and my students. I can even use several of them to give students a choice. I prefer not to use technology with these types of activities, so I would omit the graphing polynomials option, but I would consider asking the AI for more examples like the ones that I believe would work well for my students (polynomial puzzles and creating polynomial art).

If you are new to the classroom and don't feel confident making decisions on your own about which strategies are best, there are many resources to help. First, I recommend reaching out to your planning team, mentor, or other experienced teacher in your school building. They are usually eager to support a novice educator, and their experience will help you sift through the mountain of ideas that an AI prompt will often generate, helping you find the useful nuggets. If you have trouble finding someone near you to fill this role, consider tapping into the sizable teacher communities on social media networks like X (formerly Twitter; www.x.com), Facebook (https://facebook.com), and Threads (https://threads.net) to build your own personal learning network (PLN; Poth, 2023). Each of these platforms has a thriving community of tens of thousands (or more) classroom educators who can offer insight and give advice to help you choose the best output from your chatbot.

## Change It Up

How do you make this output even more useful and effective for your students' learning? We can start by being more specific about the types of activities we are looking for or the supplies that we have available:

> What are five hands-on activities that can be used to teach students about working with polynomials for ninth graders? The activities cannot include calculators, computers, tablets, or phones. They should include students moving around.

Try this one out and you'll see that the suggestions now include activities like relay races with polynomial tiles and bingo games. You know those moments when your students seem to need to be more physically active in class? With a quick prompt and a few minutes of careful review of the output, you can have easy options to meet them where they are.

## Try It Yourself

What are you waiting for? Go ask an AI chatbot to suggest some hands-on activities for your students. Did you find a way to write your prompt that resulted in really stellar output? Capture it in the following space.

## TIPS FOR TEAMS

Sometimes it can feel like the most challenging facet of working with AI is figuring out how best to craft a prompt to get the kind of output that you are looking for. That's natural, given how new this technology is, but don't let it stop you and your team from exploring what these tools can do. When you find yourself stuck, try finding an example of a product (document, image, or AI output) your team already has that is similar to what you are seeking. Perhaps one of your teammates has created something amazing for one topic, and your team would like to adapt it to other concepts that you teach. Try sharing the ideal resource with the chatbot by uploading it, and then ask it to tell you what prompt would cause it to produce this output. This is called *reverse prompt engineering* (Fagerlie, 2023), and it can give you a great starting point to create the prompt that you need. Once you have the reverse-engineered prompt, you can adjust it for other topics or situations.

## Solving Real Problems: Create Project-Based Lessons

*Project-based learning* (PBL) is a powerful method that empowers students to tackle real-world problems and use research methods, creativity, and collaborative skills to find solutions (Boss, Larmer, & Mergendoller, 2013). Because PBL involves so many important 21st century skills—critical thinking, communication, teamwork, project management, and so on—it is a technique with a really big potential for educational impact. So, why isn't it employed more often in K–12 classrooms everywhere? Research shows that the time and effort needed to create meaningful PBL lessons is likely the cause (Revelle, Wise, Duke, & Halvorsen, 2020). Sounds like a great opportunity to enlist the help of a generative AI tool, right? Try this:

> ✦ Design a complete project-based learning unit about colonialism for middle school students.

### Sample Output

Designing a complete project-based learning (PBL) unit on colonialism for middle school students involves several steps. The goal of such a unit would be to engage students in deep, hands-on learning about the historical, cultural, and social aspects of colonialism, fostering critical thinking, collaboration, and research skills. Here's a comprehensive outline for this unit:

**Unit Title**
**Exploring the Facets of Colonialism: A Journey Through History**

**Duration**
Approximately 4–6 weeks

**Key Learning Objectives**

1. **Understand the Historical Context:** Students will learn about the global history of colonialism, including the major colonial powers and the regions they colonized.

2. **Analyze Cultural and Social Impacts:** Students will explore the impact of colonialism on native cultures, societies, and economies.

3. **Develop Critical Thinking:** Through analysis and discussion, students will critically examine the consequences and legacy of colonialism.

4. **Enhance Research and Presentation Skills:** Students will conduct research, collaborate, and present their findings effectively.

**Essential Question**
"How has colonialism shaped our world, and what are its lasting impacts?"

**Project Overview**
Students will work in groups to create a comprehensive presentation on a specific aspect of colonialism. Each group will focus on a different region or theme.

**Steps**

**Week 1–2: Introduction and Research**

1. **Introduction to Colonialism:** Interactive lectures and discussions to provide a basic understanding of colonialism.

2. **Group Formation and Topic Assignment:** Students form groups and are assigned different regions/themes (for example, British colonialism in India, the cultural impact of colonialism in Africa).

3. **Initial Research:** Students start researching their assigned topics using a mix of textbooks, online resources, and library materials.

**Week 3–4: In-Depth Study and Analysis**

1. **Guest Speakers and Virtual Field Trips:** Invite experts or organize virtual visits to museums or historical sites.

2. **Workshop on Critical Analysis:** Teach students how to analyze historical events critically.

3. **Continued Group Work:** Groups delve deeper into their topics, focusing on specific aspects like economic changes, cultural shifts, resistance movements, and so on.

**Week 5: Project Development**

1. **Creating Presentations:** Each group creates a presentation, which could be in the form of a video documentary, a website, a slideshow, or a poster series.

2. **Peer Reviews:** Groups exchange their work for peer review and constructive feedback.

**Week 6: Presentation and Reflection**

1. **Presentation Day:** Each group presents their findings to the class.

2. **Class Discussion:** Postpresentation discussions to reflect on the learned material.

3. **Reflective Essays:** Each student writes a reflective essay on what they have learned and their personal views on the impacts of colonialism.

**Assessment**

Group Project (40 percent)

Participation and Engagement (20 percent)

Reflective Essay (30 percent)

Peer Review Contribution (10 percent)

**Resources Needed**

- Access to library and online academic databases
- Multimedia tools for presentations
- Guest speakers or virtual field trip arrangements

**Additional Activities**

- **Debate:** Organize a debate on a contentious issue related to colonialism.
- **Art Project:** Have students create art pieces that express their understanding or feelings about colonialism.

This PBL unit is designed to be adaptable and encourages active participation, critical thinking, and creative expression, helping students gain a multifaceted understanding of colonialism and its impacts.

It looks like the chatbot captured the overall objective of PBL, but it may need some tweaks to include the components of a good PBL lesson like the kind developed at the Buck Institute for Education (n.d.). It's a great start, but be sure to double-check that output like this from an AI tool matches the type of learning experience that you are working to create in your classroom. Remember that you can supply the bot with references to the specific strategy that you would like to use. I would paste in links to websites about PBL so that the chatbot can use them as context for better responses. Anytime you are using acronyms or abbreviations, be sure that the chatbot understands them by reviewing the output. PBL, for example, can sometimes mean *problem-based learning*. It may be helpful to spell out acronyms like these to avoid ambiguity. Once you've provided background content, you can add subsequent instructions in the same conversation and generate more PBL ideas with the same constraints.

## Change It Up

Many teachers want to incorporate elements of the PBL model for instruction but lack the time or training to implement a full project-based unit. We can use the power of the AI to help us adapt a full PBL lesson to fit the time and resources available:

> Design a project-based learning unit about colonization for middle school students that can be completed in three days. Make sure that it includes a real-world problem and a public product at the end.

If, on the other hand, you are looking for PBL components that you can combine in a more flexible way for your students, you can ask the chatbot to help you generate ideas a la carte. Sometimes, this is a great way to modify existing PBL units to teach new curriculum standards:

> Help me brainstorm ten ideas for driving questions for a PBL unit about modern art for high school students. Also, give me ten ideas for public projects at the end of the unit.

One of the strengths of these tools is their ability to analyze existing content, as I've discussed previously (Avoiding Reinventing the Wheel, page 42). If you've already used PBL with your students but had some issues, you can ask the AI for help improving a lesson that you upload or copy and paste into the prompt:

> Help me make this PBL unit better. It took too long, and students were not as interested as I wanted them to be. They didn't think the question was relevant to them.

PBL is such a powerful tool, and more teachers would probably use it if they had help designing their lessons and creating the necessary materials. You can use more high-impact strategies like this with your students if you leverage AI tools to make the work more manageable.

## Try It Yourself

Are you considering using PBL with the help of a generative AI tool? Capture your ideas and chatbot output in the following space.

----

----

----

----

----

----

----

----

----

# Flipping That Lesson: Craft Lessons That Maximize Class Time

Starting in the early 2000s and fueled by the emergence of easy-to-use tools like one-button video cameras and free video hosting sites such as YouTube, the *flipped classroom* concept took off quickly (Lage, Platt, & Treglia, 2000). The idea was to reverse (or "flip") the traditional pattern of direct instruction during class time and individual practice at home. Teachers instead would record their lessons for students to watch as homework (and sometimes paired with online discussion) before arriving in class for guided practice and small-group support from the teacher. Although the best results came from teacher-made instructional videos, much of the hype came from educator Sal Khan, whose Khan Academy videos provide detailed lessons on all sorts of topics for middle and high school students.

I jumped onto the flipped classroom bandwagon early on, but quickly found the biggest struggle was making sure that students watched the videos. Many students were not motivated to watch me droning on in a little window on their laptop at home each night, but many more didn't have the resources to watch online videos at home. Over time, I learned to shift the timing of my flipped instruction to provide in-class time for these asynchronous video lessons and differentiated practice activities that freed me to move around the classroom supporting students who needed help.

But that level of preparation, including crafting lesson videos and creating leveled practice materials, made even my modified flipped classroom model unsustainable. I just couldn't find the time to keep producing the necessary resources. Any time that a potentially impactful learning strategy is hindered by a lack of sufficient teacher time and energy, the conditions are right for AI tools to make a difference.

You can start by determining what you'll need to make a flipped classroom work for your learning space and your students. Here is a list to start with.

- Instructional videos for the direct instruction portion of each lesson
- Collaborative small-group practice activities
- Worksheets and examples to support students one on one
- Student-paced formative assessments that help students determine if they have mastered the skill or concept

Now we just need a prompt that will help us create these resources:

> ✦ **Plan out a flipped classroom lesson about persuasive writing for fifth graders. Provide scripts for video lessons, as well as materials for in-class practice.**

## Sample Output

A flipped classroom approach for teaching persuasive writing to fifth graders involves students initially learning the material at home through video lessons and then applying that knowledge in class through practical activities. Here's a plan for such a lesson:

### Video Lessons (Home Learning)

**Video Lesson 1: Introduction to Persuasive Writing**

**Duration:** 5 minutes

**Script**

- **Introduction:** "Hello, young writers! Today, we're diving into the world of persuasive writing. What is persuasive writing? It's a way to convince someone to agree with your point of view."
- **Examples:** Show examples of persuasive writing (e.g., advertisements, opinion pieces in newspapers).
- **Key Elements:** Introduce the three pillars of persuasive writing: Ethos (credibility), Pathos (emotional appeal), and Logos (logical argument).

**Video Lesson 2: Building Your Argument**

**Duration:** 7 minutes

**Script**

- **Introduction:** "Now that we know what persuasive writing is, let's learn how to build a strong argument."

- **Steps:** Explain how to choose a topic, state an opinion, and gather supporting facts or examples.

- **Interactive Element:** Pause the video at intervals and ask students to think of an opinion and one supporting fact.

**Video Lesson 3: Writing Persuasively**

**Duration:** 8 minutes

**Script**

- **Introduction:** "You've picked your topic and gathered facts. Great! Now let's put it all together."

- **Structure:** Explain the structure of a persuasive essay (introduction, body, conclusion).

- **Tips:** Offer tips on persuasive language, connecting with the audience, and counter-arguments.

## In-Class Activities (School Learning)

### Activity 1: Group Discussion

- Split students into small groups.

- Each group discusses a topic and comes up with a collective opinion.

- Encourage the use of persuasive language.

### Activity 2: Writing Workshop

- Provide worksheets with persuasive writing prompts.

- Students choose a prompt and start drafting their essays.

- Teacher moves around the room, offering guidance and feedback.

### Activity 3: Peer Review

- Students swap essays with a partner.

- They provide constructive feedback on each other's work, focusing on the use of persuasive elements.

### Activity 4: Presentation and Debate

- Students volunteer to read their essays aloud.

- After each presentation, open the floor for a polite debate.

- Encourage students to use persuasive language in their arguments and rebuttals.

### Materials for In-Class Practice

- Worksheets with persuasive writing prompts.

- Checklist for persuasive writing elements (ethos, pathos, logos, structure).

- Peer review feedback forms.

**Follow-Up**

- Assign a final persuasive essay as homework.
- Provide an online forum for students to discuss ideas and ask questions.

This flipped classroom approach ensures that students receive foundational knowledge at home, allowing more time in class for interactive and practical learning, thereby enhancing their understanding of persuasive writing.

Acknowledging that the most common chatbots cannot make the videos themselves at the time of this writing, I found the video scripts to be a good start. If I needed a more detailed script, especially if I am new to teaching this content, I could ask the AI to provide more specifics. But I would also caution that this type of video is often most effective when it has a casual style that is more approachable for students. The in-class activities are collaborative and involve a range of modalities such as creation and presentation. I also find shorter videos (less than ten minutes long) to be best for flipped instruction as it provides more chunking for students and more opportunity to pause and replay portions of the video, and the chatbot did a great job making the same recommendation.

## Change It Up

So, how do you modify this type of prompt to make it more useful in some specific situations? Well, I have found that participation in the watching of video lessons (whether it happens at home or at school) is higher when I pair students up for accountability purposes. You can help these teams by providing activities for them to do after watching the videos:

> Plan out a flipped classroom lesson about persuasive writing for fifth graders. Provide scripts for video lessons, as well as materials for in-class practice and video guide questions (and answers) for pairs of students to complete after watching each video.

If you are looking to decide which topics in your curriculum are best suited to a flipped classroom format or how best to divide the work between in class and out of class, you can ask the chatbot to provide advice:

> What topics in fourth-grade mathematics would work the best for a flipped classroom lesson?

> If I am trying to teach about the electromagnetic spectrum to high school students in a flipped classroom setting, which parts of the lesson should be completed outside of class?

Remember that in the end, you know your students and your pedagogy better than an AI chatbot, and you should always review these types of suggestions before proceeding with them.

## Try It Yourself

Whether you are new to the flipped classroom or have been using it for years, try one of these prompts and see if the output sparks your imagination. Capture your ideas in the following space.

--------------------------------------------------------------------------------

--------------------------------------------------------------------------------

--------------------------------------------------------------------------------

--------------------------------------------------------------------------------

--------------------------------------------------------------------------------

--------------------------------------------------------------------------------

--------------------------------------------------------------------------------

--------------------------------------------------------------------------------

## Explaining With Graphics: Design Visual Explanations

Up to this point, I have shared generative AI prompts that focused on text output. But alongside the rapid development of text chatbots, image-generation tools have also evolved. With some limitations, they provide amazing opportunities to create teaching visuals on demand. As these tools advance, they will become more integrated with text tools like ChatGPT and Gemini so that we will no longer need to choose our AI tools based on the type of output we are seeking.

Before diving into the creation of images, however, you need to be aware of where the AI models excel and where they fall short. All the modern image-generation models, like DALL-E and MidJourney, produce amazing original examples of visual imagery when prompted for a subject and style. Within a few seconds, they can create very lifelike people and animals, or match virtually any creative style. However, even the most advanced multimodal (text, images, music) generative AI models at the time of this writing have trouble combining images and text. Words in images are often misspelled or written in undecipherable gibberish. This is mostly because the AI was designed with images as its primary training corpus and image creation as its purpose.

As a result of these limitations, you'll get the best results if you include lots of details when you prompt an image-generation AI model. Be prepared to have inaccurate or even indecipherable text included. Since the AI can't really "see" the text it is generating, it is frequently not able to exclude or remove it. Here is an example:

> ✦ Make a simple diagram that shows the parts of the human digestive
> system. Make it easily accessible to elementary school students
> and somewhat realistic. Use colors and shading to make the
> diagram appealing and easy to understand.

### Sample Output

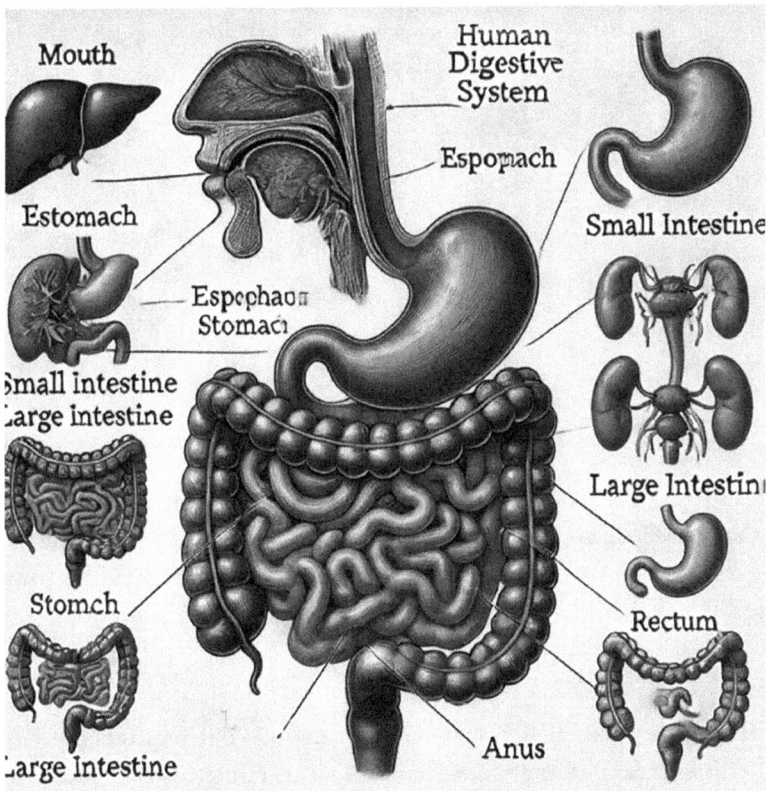

*Source: Image generated by DALL-E 3 through ChatGPT, July 8, 2024.*

Right away, it's clear that the AI doesn't really understand the content that it is creating. This image is a classic example of the good (simple, easily reproducible image generated quickly) and the bad (misspelled words, inaccurate labels) that comes with using image-generation tools to make educational infographics. You can use some prompt modifications to minimize the errors, but it is often impossible to generate a diagram without any text. Most diagrams used to train the model had text on them (Mirjalili, 2023), and the model doesn't know how to isolate it and remove it. You may find yourself needing to use image-editing software, such as Adobe Photoshop or Canva (www.canva.com), to change the text on the image after it's generated.

If we instead prompt the chatbot to create an image for a topic with fewer labeled parts and ask for *examples* rather than a *diagram*, the results improve considerably.

> ✦✦  **Make image examples of clothing styles from the 1980s.**

### Sample Output

*Source: Image generated by DALL-E 3 through ChatGPT, July 12, 2024.*

For this topic, the AI created exactly what a teacher might be looking for: usable content that is visually appealing and demonstrates the concepts well. The challenge is providing the chatbot with enough details and instruction to create the type of visual that you are seeking, which will be easier for some course content than for others.

## Change It Up

I've already demonstrated how much more explicit our prompts need to be when working with images. But sometimes the AI model can infer what we need from a simpler statement. The best way to generate these visual explanations is to start simple and add more detail as needed:

> ✦✦  **Make an image without words that demonstrates the idea of foreshadowing.**

## Sample Output

*Source: Image generated by DALL-E 3 through ChatGPT, December 13, 2023.*

Here, the output meets my needs right away. But what if you wanted something more complex?

> ✦ Make an image without words that demonstrates how ocean currents work.

## Sample Output

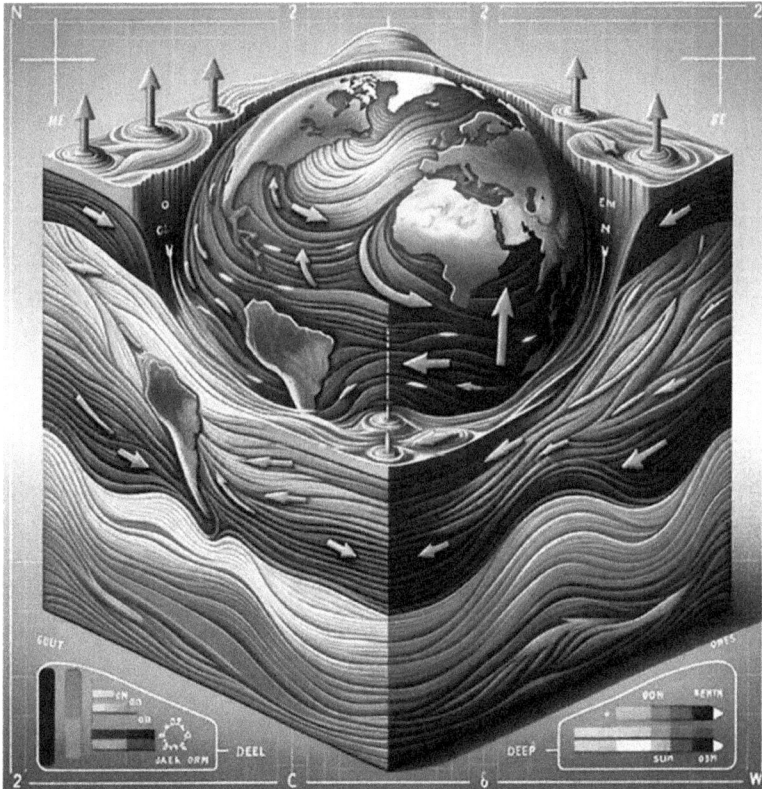

*Source: Image generated by DALL-E 3 through ChatGPT, December 13, 2023.*

While this graphic is very visually appealing, its abstract design makes it difficult for students to understand anything new about ocean currents by looking at it. In fact, some of the elements of the graphic are simply inaccurate. It even includes gibberish text, despite the prompt asking for no text.

So, how do we modify our prompt to get a more useful graphic? We need to be more specific and force the chatbot to remove unnecessary details that might be artistic but not factual:

> ✦✦ Make a simple and realistic diagram without words that shows how surface ocean currents are caused by wind.

**Sample Output**

*Source: Image generated by DALL-E 3 through ChatGPT, December 13, 2023.*

This output is much more useful in the classroom because it more accurately represents the flow of water in a clear way without words. Its simplicity helps it avoid providing inaccurate information. By adding labels (using a tool like Canva) or adjacent explanatory text, teachers can use an image like this to make a lesson more visual and engaging for students.

As you can see, the image-generation AI tools that exist at this time are more suited to creating visuals for lessons in the humanities than they are for scientific illustrations. Keep that in mind when experimenting with these prompts.

## Try It Yourself

Consider a topic from your content and try some of these prompt examples. Customize them to get clear and accurate visuals. Write down what worked in the following space.

-------------------------------------------------------------------------------

-------------------------------------------------------------------------------

-------------------------------------------------------------------------------

-------------------------------------------------------------------------------

-------------------------------------------------------------------------------

-------------------------------------------------------------------------------

-------------------------------------------------------------------------------

-------------------------------------------------------------------------------

# Using Stories as Examples: Create Relevant Case Studies

Case studies are a highly effective way to help students understand topics that have clear applications to the real world. They present students with realistic examples of what they are learning about and give them a chance to work collaboratively to learn more (Schwartz, 2019). In addition, when students explore case studies, they often do not all reach the same conclusion or recommendation for future action. This can lead to broader perspectives for students and the opportunity for discussion and debate.

Historically, case studies have been challenging to create because they require time and expertise, as well as strong knowledge of the underlying processes. While teachers have the necessary content knowledge, we often do not have the time needed to make these powerful resources. Let's put the AI to work closing that gap:

> ✦✦ **Create a case study that would be used to teach high school students about personal finance.**

## Sample Output

### Case Study: Planning for the Future—The Story of Alex and Jordan

### Background

Alex, aged 17, and Jordan, aged 18, are high school seniors planning for their future after graduation. Alex has been working a part-time job and saving money, while Jordan has just started thinking about financial planning.

### Scenario

Alex has $5,000 saved from their part-time job and wants to manage this money wisely. Alex plans to attend a local community college next year and needs to budget for tuition, books, and personal expenses. Alex's parents have agreed to cover half of the tuition.

Jordan, on the other hand, has no savings but has just secured a part-time job. Jordan dreams of traveling for a year before attending college and is unsure how to finance this plan.

### Objectives

1. **Budgeting:** Create a monthly budget for Alex, considering their income, college expenses, and personal expenses.

2. **Saving and Investing:** Advise Alex on how to use their $5,000 savings effectively.

3. **Debt Management:** Discuss how Jordan can avoid high-interest debt while planning for their gap year.

4. **Income Planning:** Help Jordan create a plan to save enough money for their travels and future college expenses.

### Questions for Discussion

For Alex:

- How should Alex allocate their savings between immediate college expenses and longer-term savings?

- What are some cost-effective strategies for managing daily expenses while in college?

- Are there any investment options suitable for Alex's short-term and long-term goals?

For Jordan:

- What financial strategies should Jordan adopt to save for the gap year?

- How can Jordan balance the desire to travel with the need to save for college?

- What are the risks of using credit cards or loans to fund the gap year travel?

**Additional Tasks**

- **Research Assignment:** Investigate different types of savings accounts and investment options available to young adults.

- **Group Activity:** Role-play a financial advising session where one student is Alex or Jordan and another is a financial advisor.

- **Presentation:** Create a financial plan presentation for either Alex or Jordan, showcasing budgeting, saving, and investment strategies.

**Conclusion**

This case study aims to teach students about the importance of budgeting, saving, investing, and managing debt at a young age. Through Alex and Jordan's scenarios, students can learn to apply these principles to their own lives, preparing them for financial independence and responsibility.

This output includes basic questions and a solid explanation of the why behind this sort of learning activity. You should always look carefully to ensure close alignment of a larger lesson like this with your learning targets and edit the output (or adjust the prompt) to make it fit well.

## Change It Up

There are many ways to direct an AI chatbot to generate this type of content for your classroom. In addition to changing the topic and the grade level, it's also easy to get the AI to produce more detailed documents to help you:

> Create a case study for sixth graders to study soil quality set in rural Oklahoma with characters names Juan and Quantia. Include a teacher's guide and create the handouts for the students to complete.

The output from this modified prompt will provide text that you can cut and paste into a blank word-processing document to create the necessary student papers. Perhaps instead you would like to use a case study with a hybrid or online-only class. You can modify the prompt to meet those parameters:

> Create a case study for sixth graders to study soil quality set in rural Oklahoma with characters names Juan and Quantia. Include a teacher's guide and suggestions for making the lesson work in an online-only learning environment.

## Try It Yourself

Do you teach any concepts that students could learn through collaborative discussion of a real-world case study? Brainstorm some ideas and capture them in the following space.

----------------------------------------

----------------------------------------

----------------------------------------

----------------------------------------

----------------------------------------

----------------------------------------

# Getting in the Game: Generate Ideas for Simulation Games

One of the most powerful ways for students to grapple with complex processes is to use simulations to observe them and the effects of different inputs on them (Campos, Nogal, Caliz, & Juan, 2020). While computer programs can make very powerful simulations, many of my favorite simulations are decidedly low-tech. I find that students better grasp the forces at play in processes like natural selection and food webs when they can have a tangible experience with dice, tokens, and other manipulatives.

Using simulations, though, is a big task. Teachers need to brainstorm the best ways to simulate a complex or abstract idea. Then, they need to produce the rules and other components of the simulation game. A carefully worded chatbot prompt can allow an AI model to do the heavy lifting for us:

> ✦ What are three ideas for simulation games (without computers) that can be used to help second-grade students understand how animals change and develop during their lifetime?

### Sample Output

1. **Life-Cycle Relay Race**

    Objective: Understand animal life-cycle stages through a relay race.

    Materials: Life-cycle stage cards, cones

    Instructions: Teams race, passing cards for each life stage (for example, egg, larva, adult). Discuss stages after the race.

2. **Animal Growth Chart Activity**

   Objective: Visualize animal growth over time.

   Materials: Large paper, markers, animal stage pictures

   Instructions: Students draw animals at different growth stages on a chart, then present and discuss size and appearance changes.

3. **Metamorphosis Role-Play**

   Objective: Act out metamorphosis to understand transformation.

   Materials: Costumes or props for stages (for example, wings, antennae)

   Instructions: Students role-play each metamorphosis stage (e.g., egg, caterpillar, butterfly) with movements and props. Discuss the process afterward.

As you look over the list of choices, you can think about your students' interests and your classroom culture, as well as the amount of time that you can allot to one of these activities. For example, I might choose option 2 because I like the idea of students drawing the animals and then taking turns performing the changes for other members of the class. Or I might choose option 1 or 3 if I prefer that students move around. I love the idea of the life-cycle stage cards from the first option because they can be a great visual option for less proficient readers.

## Change It Up

There are many ways to adapt this type of prompt. For example, you can ask for ideas that are better suited to larger classes or for students who need additional academic support:

> ✦ **What are five ideas for simulation games (without computers) that can be used to help second-grade students who are struggling readers to understand how animals change and develop during their lifetime?**

> ✦ **What are five ideas for simulation games (without computers) that can be used in large classes of twenty-five or more students to help second-grade students understand how animals change and develop during their lifetime?**

You'll find that these modified prompts generate game suggestions that include additional elements to fit the unique requirements of each classroom situation, such as more visual games for students who need reading supports or stations around the classroom to meet the challenges of larger classes.

## Try It Yourself

Use an AI chatbot to find a topic that you teach that is well suited for a simulation game and check out the suggestions that it provides. Record your favorite in the following space.

------

------

------

------

------

------

# Chapter Reflection

The point in a learning cycle when students receive the opportunity to interact with new content is what many people picture when they imagine *teaching*. While in the past, this might have taken the form of a teacher-centered lecture, extensive research has shown us more effective ways to transfer knowledge. We know now that the more interactive and collaborative the lesson, the more likely students are to engage with it and incorporate new ideas into their thinking.

With so many ways to present new information to students, the biggest challenge for teachers is often being aware of all the options and deciding which modalities and strategies will yield the best results. The search for a better way to teach a topic frequently takes up more of our time than the lessons themselves. But AI holds the potential to act as an assistant that performs the research and presents the options so that classroom educators can exercise our professional judgment in choosing and implementing what's best for our students.

In this chapter, we looked at AI prompts that help teachers better connect students with new ideas (Explaining It Better and Explaining with Graphics) and avoid starting from scratch (Avoiding Reinventing the Wheel). We also looked at how chatbots can generate the pieces of great direct instruction (Leaning Into Literacy and Scripting Your Presentation) and more inquiry-based learning (Getting Their Hands Dirty, Solving Real Problems, Flipping That Lesson, Using Stories as Examples, and Getting in the Game). Throughout the chapter, we focused on how AI models can lower the barrier to entry so that you can make positive changes to your instruction that will help every one of your students learn more.

Next, let's explore how to use AI to help students practice and review what they have learned.

# Chapter 2 Questions for Discussion

What is a friction point for you and your students when you present new content? Which of the prompts in this chapter feel like they will help with this issue?

What is a strategy that you use in your classroom instruction that you would like to revamp with some AI help? How do you think that learning in your class would be different with that help?

What is an instructional task that you find tedious or time-consuming? How do you think an AI chatbot could help?

# CHAPTER 3

# Reinforcing and Reviewing

✦ "I'm ready." That's what a quirky eighth grader named Orlando would always say to me when he had finished taking notes or watching a science video. "Ready for what?" I always asked. "The test, Mr. C," was his usual response. "I want to take the test while I can still remember what I just learned."

Learning is often considered in the public imagination as simply the commitment of facts to memory. Many adults recall the use of rote memorization as the primary method of teaching during their days in school. However, with the help of brain research and a more holistic understanding of what it means to learn something, the field of education has embraced the idea that skills develop through cycles of practice and feedback (Czerkawski, 2014). We know that lessons that present new skills and information to students need to be followed with opportunities to practice those skills in a variety of ways.

This reinforcement element in the learning process is what helps create synaptic pathways and facilitates long-term recall. It also deepens students' understanding of complex ideas, shifting from memorization to comprehension (Forsberg, Adams, & Cowan, 2021). This level of mastery is what allows students to solve complex problems and apply their learning to new situations. Employers are increasingly seeking individuals with these skills for better-paying jobs (Flaherty, 2021; McGarry, 2016).

The availability of personalized and actionable feedback is a critical part of any reinforcement of learning. Through this feedback, students identify their weaknesses, improve their mastery of a topic, and gain confidence in their abilities. It's not just a nice extra step to the learning process—it's the critical point where exploration becomes knowledge.

But we also know that our students are more varied than ever—in their learning needs, strengths and weaknesses, and interests. Moreover, educators recognize more than ever the importance of acknowledging the variety of students' educational histories, family backgrounds, and personal identities. We need to ensure that the opportunities that we create for the reinforcement of learning are just as varied. Brainstorming and build-ing these activities can be a heavy lift for busy teachers, but as we have already seen, AI chatbots are well suited to partner with educators for this task. In this chapter, you will explore ten prompts that help teachers facilitate practice that leads to mastery.

## Saying *Yes SIR*: Spaced Repeating, Interleaving, and Retrieving

I used to bristle at the idea that I need to teach my students how to study for assess-ments. I like to believe that, if I've done my job well, they will "just know" what they need to know. But the truth is that many students do not have the skills to study effectively.

The good news is that we know what works. Tons of education research from the worlds of professional training, higher education, and now K–12 has shown the power of using a combination of three strategies to encourage long-term capture of important information in memory (Sana & Yan, 2022; Thompson & Hughes, 2023).

1. **Spaced repetition:** This is the simple technique of slowly increasing the time between practice sessions with the same content. Research has demonstrated that this increases the speed at which knowledge and skills are transferred to long-term memory (Kang, 2016).

2. **Interleaving:** Rather than spending study sessions focused on a single topic, experimental results suggest that it is more effective to alternate different topics. This seems to force the brain to be more flexible and keep multiple ideas accessible (Thompson & Hughes, 2023).

3. **Retrieval practice:** Many studies have tested the idea that passively looking over notes and other captured learning content can be as effective as students actively testing themselves by trying to recall what they've learned. The results are crystal clear—actively recalling learned ideas is much more powerful than just browsing one's notes (Agarwal, D'Antonio, Roediger, McDermott, & McDaniel, 2014).

Taken together, these three strategies are often abbreviated with the acronym *SIR*. So, if we know that using one or more of these techniques helps our students to be able to recall what they have learned, why don't we teach them how to use them and give them practice in class? Here's a prompt to try:

> ✦ **Create three activities that will help my tenth-grade students study for a test on the Renaissance using spaced repetition, interleaving, and retrieval practice.**

### Sample Output

To help your tenth-grade students study for a test on the Renaissance using spaced repetition, interleaving, and retrieval practice, you can design a variety of engaging and effective activities. Here are three suggestions.

- **Renaissance Timeline Construction:** Over a week, assign students to create a timeline of key Renaissance events, adding a few each day. This activity uses spaced repetition as they review and add new information daily. To integrate interleaving, mix in review of previous history topics related to the Renaissance.

- **Art and Innovator Flashcards:** Students create flashcards featuring Renaissance artists, innovators, and their works. These cards are used for daily short review sessions, employing spaced repetition. To incorporate interleaving, mix cards from different disciplines (art, science, politics) in each session.

- **Group Quizzes With Rotating Topics:** Organize weekly group quizzes where the topic changes each session (for example, Renaissance art one week, scientific advancements the next). This uses retrieval practice by testing their knowledge and interleaving by switching between topics.

These activities engage students in active learning, helping them to better retain and understand the Renaissance period through varied and repeated exposure to the material.

If you're not sure how to get started with any of these three strategies, this list is a perfect first step. I really like that the chatbot explains which technique—spaced repetition, interleaving, or retrieval practice—is being used in each example. Notice that the flashcards in option 2 can showcase both spaced repetition and interleaving, giving you even more bang for your buck. As with many brainstorming lists like this one, there are some activities on this list that I would use and others that are not a good fit for my students or my situation.

## Change It Up

Of course, if you would prefer to focus on a single topic that you are teaching or on one of the three SIR strategies, you can modify the prompt to get more specific output:

> **Create five activities that will help my tenth-grade students review the artists of the Dada movement using spaced repetition.**

If you are just starting to use SIR study strategies with your students, you can use the generative AI chatbot to help you create short activities that explain the strategies and demonstrate the effectiveness of each one:

> **I want to teach my students how to use spaced repetition to study more efficiently. Create a handout that will explain the strategy to them, including its rationale. Also include a short activity that shows my students how powerful this strategy is.**

## Try It Yourself

Do you think that your students need more help learning how to study effectively? Do you think that the SIR strategies might help them? Capture your thinking in the following space.

--------------------------------------------------------------------------------

--------------------------------------------------------------------------------

--------------------------------------------------------------------------------

--------------------------------------------------------------------------------

--------------------------------------------------------------------------------

--------------------------------------------------------------------------------

--------------------------------------------------------------------------------

--------------------------------------------------------------------------------

--------------------------------------------------------------------------------

--------------------------------------------------------------------------------

## Questioning the Image: Create Learning Activities From Diagrams and Art

One of my favorite ways to reinforce new lessons is to expose my students to the same ideas in many different formats. Visual representations are especially effective media for this purpose (Cook, 2006; Tippett, 2016). Often, as an educator, you come across a diagram or infographic that helpfully explains a concept from your class. You want your students to investigate the graphic, interpret the data that it represents, and draw conclusions. Or, if you teach the humanities or arts, you may want students to interpret pieces of artwork or examples of political cartoons, looking for their meaning or significance and connecting it to the concepts you are teaching in your class.

The good news is that as of this writing, generative AI chatbots have the ability to recognize specific patterns in uploaded images and summarize them, analyze them, or create learning activities around them. In the same location where you enter your prompt, you can upload or attach an image file, or simply copy and paste the image file (with a keystroke or a right-click) directly into the prompt line. Let's give it a try:

> ✦ **Create a five-question guide to accompany this image of a piece of Cheyenne artwork that asks ninth-grade students about purpose and significance.**
>
>
>
> *Source: Anonymous (possibly Cheyenne), ca. 1890. Artwork is in the public domain.*

## Sample Output

To accompany the image of Cheyenne artwork, a five-question guide for ninth-grade students could be:

1. What visual elements does the artist use to convey movement in this piece of Cheyenne ledger art?

2. Discuss the possible symbolic significance of the horse in Cheyenne culture as represented in this artwork.

3. How does the use of color contribute to the overall meaning or feeling of this artwork? Are there any patterns in the color usage that stand out to you?

4. Ledger art often tells a story or records events. What story or event do you think is being depicted in this image? What details in the drawing support your interpretation?

5. Compare and contrast this artwork with another form of narrative art you have studied. How does the medium (ledger paper versus canvas, wall, and so on) affect the way the story is told or the way the artwork is perceived?

Isn't it helpful that the chatbot can "see" the content of the image and produce useful questions as a result? It is a powerful activity to reinforce the concepts of 19th century Native American life and art. Once you've reviewed the AI-generated questions, you may decide to use them as they are. Of course, you can modify the questions as necessary to match the learning targets and rigor level that you're looking for.

## Change It Up

Asking the AI to craft questions for you when you have a useful image is helpful, but what if you need help understanding the image that you have found? Political cartoons can sometimes be challenging for students and educators alike. Often, though, a well-trained chatbot can help you learn more:

**What is the message of this political cartoon? How might I use this to reinforce for my students the two sides of the issue of the Red Scare?**

*Source: Berryman, 1919. Artwork is in the public domain.*

The output from a prompt like this would include specific elements of the political cartoon to point out to students, as well as ideas for classroom discussion. Remember that the depth and complexity of the response—as well as the ease of including the photo—may vary between AI models (free versus premium). This type of analysis works best with images that reference more widely known events and issues. And remember that you can also ask the chatbot to provide answers to any questions that it creates.

## Try It Yourself

Give this prompt a try by finding an image (photo, cartoon, graph, infographic, and so on) and uploading it to an AI chatbot with a prompt to explain the image, summarize the image, or create useful student assignments from it. Record your reflection in the following space.

---------------------------------------------------------------------

---------------------------------------------------------------------

---------------------------------------------------------------------

---------------------------------------------------------------------

---------------------------------------------------------------------

---------------------------------------------------------------------

# Doing the Math: Generating Mathematics Word Problems

One of the biggest roadblocks for mathematics teachers who want to give their students more practice problems is the time it takes to generate them. In the past, teachers would need pages and pages of sample problems from workbooks or textbooks or handouts from other teachers. With the availability of the internet, teachers might get lucky and find useful problems through a web search. AI has changed this completely, providing mathematics teachers with any number of problems to practice any skill at any grade level:

> **Generate three word problems for fifth-grade students to practice probability.**

### Sample Output

Sure, here are three word problems suitable for fifth-grade students to practice probability.

1. **School Library Books:** The school library has 40 books. Twenty of these are fiction, 10 are nonfiction, and the rest are comic books. If a student randomly selects a book to read, what is the probability that the book is a comic book?

2. **Marble Bag:** Emma has a bag of marbles containing 5 red marbles, 10 blue marbles, and 15 green marbles. If Emma picks a marble at random, what is the probability that she will pick a red marble?

3. **Classroom Birthdays:** In a classroom of 30 students, 6 students have birthdays in January, 8 have birthdays in May, and the rest have birthdays in other months. If a student is chosen at random, what is the probability that this student has a birthday in May?

When looking over the output from a prompt like this, I start by verifying the accuracy of the mathematics calculations, as some models can still struggle with this (Bailey, 2024). Next, I check the appropriateness of the questions for my students. Can my students read these easily? Are the calculations doable for them? Is there anything missing that my students need to know? Then, I make changes to the questions to make them fit my needs better. As I mentioned in chapter 2 (page 41), don't forget about the value of your PLN to help you make these decisions.

## Change It Up

There are also some easy tweaks that you can apply to the prompt itself that can make the output even more powerful. As I discussed in chapter 1 (Making It Personal, page 30), you can make the word problems more relevant for students by including more personal details, like this:

> Generate three word problems for fifth-grade students to practice probability. Set the problems in the city of Chicago and include people named Jabar, Desiree, Caleb, and Emily.

Since the goal of the questions is to give every student more practice with the skills that they are learning, and your classroom likely includes a variety of reading skill levels, why not create several versions of each word problem?

> Generate three word problems for fifth-grade students to practice probability. For each word problem, create a grade-level version, a version at a simpler reading level, and one at a higher reading level.

To build more independence in your students, you can also ask the chatbot to create a feedback sheet that gives the correct answer to each question and explains how it can be solved. This gives students and families the tools to check their work and some support in persevering through challenging problems:

> Generate three word problems for fifth-grade students to practice probability. For each problem, include the answer and a short explanation.

## Try It Yourself

Do you teach mathematics? Give these prompts a try and capture your own tweaks in the following space. If you don't teach mathematics, share these prompts with your favorite mathematics teacher.

--------------------------------------------------------

--------------------------------------------------------

--------------------------------------------------------

--------------------------------------------------------

--------------------------------------------------------

--------------------------------------------------------

--------------------------------------------------------

# Giving Them Choice: Planning and Creating Menus, Choice Boards, and Playlists

With the growth of blended learning and student-centered learning strategies (Drysdale, Graham, Spring, & Halverson, 2013), more teachers are crafting learning experiences in which students have some control. Sometimes, this takes the form of instructional units in which students choose from a menu of different lessons and activities based on their interests or their preferences. Other times, they have a playlist of lessons to complete in whatever order and at whatever pace is appropriate for the student. My students tell me that they enjoy the opportunity to have a choice in their learning, and they respond positively when I offer them choice boards or tic-tac-toe projects, in which students choose three tasks from among nine options to complete a row.

One major obstacle to teachers offering more choice to their students is the increased amount of content that must be created. Providing options to students has powerfully positive effects on motivation and the development of executive function and decision-making skills (Vandas, Westfall, & Duvall, 2023), but it does require teachers to create multiple additional activities. To balance this additional workload and get those benefits of engagement and student ownership, let's use an AI chatbot to help us:

> Create a tic-tac-toe board of student learning and practice activities that centers on how central message and moral are portrayed in folktales and myths for third graders. Ensure that no matter which three activities students choose to complete, they will have an equitable experience.

**Sample Output**

Creating a tic-tac-toe board of student learning and practice activities for third graders focusing on the central message and moral in folktales and myths is a great idea. Here's how you can structure it:

**Tic-Tac-Toe Board: Central Message and Moral in Folktales and Myths**

**Row 1**

1. **Read and Reflect:** Read a folktale and write a paragraph about its central message.

2. **Character Interview:** Pretend to interview a character from a myth. What moral lessons did they learn?

3. **Story Mapping:** Create a story map of a folktale, highlighting key events that reveal the moral.

**Row 2**

1. **Compare and Contrast:** Choose two folktales and compare their central messages.

2. **Creative Rewrite:** Rewrite the ending of a myth to reflect a different moral.

3. **Illustrate a Scene:** Draw a scene from a folktale that best represents its central message.

**Row 3**

1. **Act It Out:** Perform a scene from a myth with a group, focusing on its moral.

2. **Storyteller's Corner:** Tell a folktale to the class, emphasizing its central message.

3. **Moral Discovery:** Choose a folktale and list the different morals it teaches.

Each of these activities touches on different aspects of learning, such as reading comprehension, critical thinking, creativity, and presentation skills. By choosing any three activities, students will get a rounded experience in understanding and interpreting the morals and central messages in folktales and myths. This approach ensures that they engage with the material in diverse and equitable ways, suitable for their grade level.

When looking at multifaceted output like this one, I try to ensure that the AI-generated activities are varied and that they can be completed in my classroom with easily obtained supplies. I think that the output shows a strong diversity of activities that will be equally challenging for students, although only the "Act It Out" activity (row 3, activity 1) is group based. If you are looking for more group or collaborative activities, be sure to specify that in your follow-up prompts. Some of these examples would also require you to have reading passages available or ask the chatbot to create them for you.

## Change It Up

There are many reasons to modify the preceding sample prompt, including adjusting the number and rigor of activities. But it also is important to remember that after working with the chatbot to brainstorm the activities, you can put it to work making drafts of the needed handouts and instruction sets:

> Create a menu of ten activities that students could do to practice how central message and moral are portrayed in folktales and myths for third graders. Make sure that each activity can be completed in fifteen minutes or less and requires nothing more than a pencil and paper.

And, after viewing the output, follow up by asking the chatbot to help you by creating drafts of several necessary documents:

> Create the student handout and instructions for activities 1, 4, and 6.

Sometimes, you want a playlist in which the activities form a progression:

> Create a playlist of five activities that sixth-grade students can do independently to practice the skills of adding and subtracting fractions. The activities should build on one another.

Remember that these types of learning experiences are best suited to situations when students will be working at their own pace, allowing you to move around the classroom checking in and providing support as needed.

## Try It Yourself

Do you think students would benefit from a set of activities for a topic that you teach? Do you want to give your students more choice and control? Use the following space to list some places in your curriculum where you think this would work.

-----------------------------------------------------------------------

-----------------------------------------------------------------------

-----------------------------------------------------------------------

-----------------------------------------------------------------------

-----------------------------------------------------------------------

## TIPS FOR TEAMS

As you explore what AI chatbots can do for you and your team, you may find that it takes several prompts in a conversation before the AI begins to give you output that matches your expectations. Teams can use specific priming statements to put their chatbot in the right "mindset" to generate more useful output:

> You are a longtime member of an instructional team of master teachers who have already developed high-quality common lessons and assessments in the past.

Or, prepare the chatbot for the diversity of your teaching team:

> You are a master teacher who is part of a team that includes several novice educators and one for whom English is a second language. Your suggestions should include this perspective.

With your team, experiment with statements like these at the start of new conversations. Look at how differently primed prompts result in different output. Be sure to write down the role statements that worked for you. And, to maximize your ability to collaborate, keep these best prompt practices in a shared document that the entire team can access and edit.

## Showing Me the Data: Make Datasets and Graphs

Analyzing data is an important skill and highly motivating learning activity in a variety of subjects from science, technology, engineering, and mathematics (STEM) fields to social sciences (Makarevitch, Frechette, & Wiatros, 2015). Students get the opportunity to see the connection between the real world and the concepts that they are studying in class, from biological processes to environmental changes to population dynamics. They can practice critical thinking as well as collaboration and communication skills if the activities are well designed. Perhaps most important, students who analyze data in class are developing the mental muscles that they will need for most of their future careers in this digital age.

Like so many other high-impact teaching strategies, however, data-analysis lessons are challenging for teachers to create. We need to find existing datasets or create our own, and we need the data within them to be both realistic and demonstrative of the concepts that we are trying to teach. We also need to ensure that they have appropriate levels of complexity to match the developmental stages of our students. As you may expect at this point, generative AI tools are uniquely proficient at this task and present a powerful way to craft exactly the resources that we need:

> Generate a dataset that demonstrates that fewer organisms are found in deeper ocean waters. The variables should be depth and number of individual organisms found.

## Sample Output

I have created a dataset and a corresponding plot that demonstrates the relationship between ocean depth and the number of individual organisms found. In this simulation:

- The depths range from the surface (0 meters) to deep ocean waters (10,000 meters).

- The number of organisms is modeled to decrease exponentially with increasing depth, indicating fewer organisms in deeper waters.

Here's a snippet of the dataset.

| Depth (Meters) | Number of Organisms |
|----------------|---------------------|
| 0.00 | 1000.00 |
| 101.01 | 950.75 |
| 202.02 | 903.92 |
| 303.03 | 859.40 |
| 404.04 | 817.08 |

And the plot visually represents this relationship, showing a clear decline in the number of organisms as depth increases.

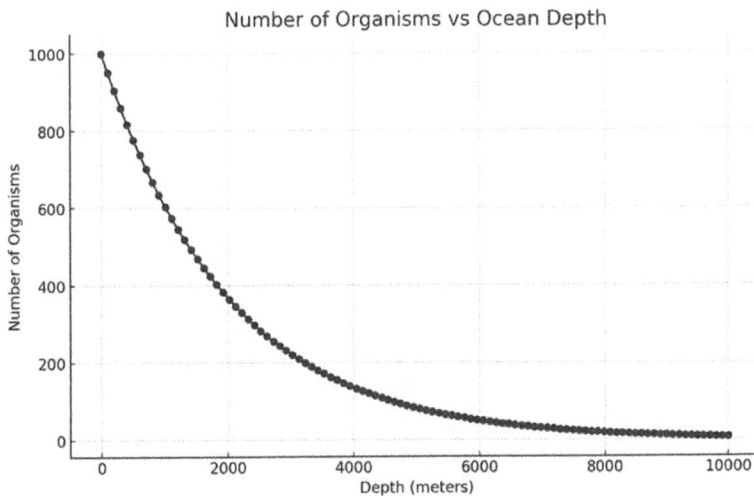

Number of Organisms vs Ocean Depth

While I am always impressed when a generative AI model creates useful content for my classroom, the output from a prompt like this one is surprisingly helpful. Some models will include the graph, and others will only offer numerical values. It's also important to recognize that these "synthetic" data are not to be confused with actual recordings from real-world situations. Consider labeling them as such before sharing them with students or colleagues for transparency and clarity. In this case, the chatbot was able to determine what a reasonable range of *x* and *y* values would be, and it generated a graph to accompany the data. The original output even included a link to the full dataset so that it can be shared with students as part of a learning activity. I have omitted the link here in the book to avoid confusion.

Where was this first prompt lacking? I found that the values fit too well to the pattern that I asked for. The data are missing the sort of normal variation that we would expect. The full dataset was also provided as a bit of computer code (in the Python language) rather than a CSV (comma separated values, a simple and universal spreadsheet format) file or Excel spreadsheet. These limitations can be easily addressed by tweaking the prompt.

## Change It Up

Let's start by adding some natural variation to the dataset. This makes it much more similar to the real world and also challenges students to recognize a pattern that might be somewhat hidden:

> ✦ Generate a dataset that demonstrates a normal distribution of heights within a population of middle school boys. Add some variation to ensure that the fit is not perfect.

**Sample Output**

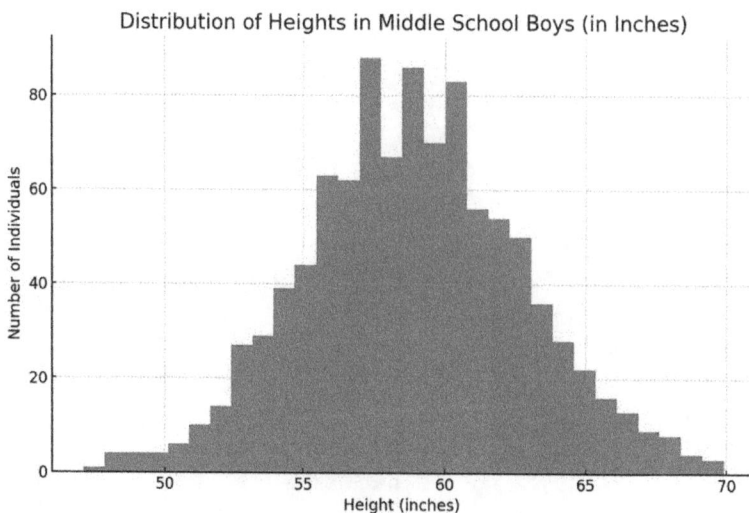

Distribution of Heights in Middle School Boys (in Inches)

Notice how the data follow a normal (bell curve) distribution but not perfectly? You might wonder why we wouldn't just measure the heights of our students for an activity like this. The answer is that the patterns that we wish to investigate often do not appear until the datasets get quite large. But I would definitely have my students compare the distribution of heights in our class to the dataset as part of this exercise.

If you want to give your students raw data that they can practice analyzing and graphing, you just need to make another small change to the prompt:

> Generate a dataset that demonstrates the amount of oxygen in the atmosphere at different altitudes from the ground up to the edge of the atmosphere. Provide the data in a spreadsheet format.

The output from this prompt included two important details. First, the chatbot provided a link to a CSV file. Second, it cautioned that the data were fabricated using expected patterns and did not represent actual measurements. This is an important point to share with students—these are simulated data—that can lead to later comparison with actual measurements like those published by a government agency.

## Try It Yourself

Do you teach a subject that includes a discussion of data? Try to identify several ways that a simulated dataset could be used in your class to enhance relevance and student engagement and record them in the following space. If you can't think of a way to use this prompt in your class, try asking a chatbot for suggested applications in your course.

## Answering "How Can I Use This?": Identify Practical Applications of Classroom Concepts

The most common question I hear from my middle school students is usually about why they need to learn a particular skill or study a specific topic. Relevance is an important element of student motivation, especially in the middle and high school grades (Schmidt, Kafkas, Maier, Shumow, & Kackar-Cam, 2019). And building student awareness of real-world and career-based applications of classroom lessons is a powerful way to get them more interested in their own learning. I find that this future focus reinforces my students' motivation.

Some teachers already have a clear sense of how their curriculum connects with job skills or life skills that students will need later. But for many subject areas and for some specific lessons, it can be difficult to communicate these connections in a way that inspires students. Let's use an AI chatbot to make the job easier:

> ✦ **What are five jobs or careers in which a person would need to be able to perform arithmetic with fractions?**

### Sample Output

Certainly! Here are five key careers where proficiency in arithmetic with fractions is especially important.

1. **Chef or Baker:** Requires precise measurement and adjustment of ingredients, often involving fractional quantities.

2. **Carpenter or Woodworker:** Involves accurate measurement and cutting of materials using fractions for lengths and angles.

3. **Pharmacist:** Calculates dosages and mixes medications, frequently using fractions to ensure correct proportions.

4. **Engineer (various fields):** Engineering tasks often require detailed calculations with fractions for design and construction purposes.

5. **Financial Analyst or Accountant:** Deals with financial data including fractional percentages like interest rates and investment returns.

This is a great, simple list that I can use to kickstart a conversation with my students about when they might use these skills in the future. I could even incorporate these jobs into a bulletin board or project in the future to reinforce the importance of the related skills.

## Change It Up

If you have already gotten to know your students, you may have some insight about the careers that they are interested in. Or you may just be familiar with high-interest jobs for the age group that you work with. With a simple adjustment to the prompt, we can generate a list of skills that are needed by workers in a particular field or a specific career:

> ✦✦ What are the middle school language arts skills that are most useful to a professional basketball player?

> ✦✦ How would a landscaper use trigonometry in their work?

I find that the output from prompts like these is highly relevant for students and can often help a student who is disinterested in a lesson.

## Try It Yourself

Do you teach a topic that sometimes gets you eye-rolls and apathy from some of your students? Try some of these prompts and record the results in the following space.

---

---

---

---

---

---

---

---

---

---

# Talking About It: Craft Meaningful and Engaging Discussion Prompts

Discussion is one of the teaching strategies that Marzano's (2017) research finds most effective (Larson, 2000). Students who discuss what they have learned—in person or online—are more likely to clear up misconceptions, develop a deeper understanding of the content, and build more supportive relationships with other students. They build confidence as they explain their thinking to others, and they often become peer teachers in the process.

Even with these benefits in mind, however, conducting discussions in your class can be tough. It often takes more time for students to learn in this format. It also creates logistical and monitoring challenges for teachers who need to ensure that students are accountable for what they add to the conversation. To make this learning format more useful for teachers, we can use an AI chatbot to help us generate expectations and a discussion question:

> ✦✦ I want my tenth-grade students to use an online discussion board to learn more about the causes of the First World War. Create a set of guidelines and expectations for the discussion and three prompts to start it.

## Sample Output

Certainly! Creating guidelines for an online discussion board is a great way to ensure a constructive and respectful exchange of ideas among your tenth-grade students. Here are some guidelines and three prompts to initiate the discussion about the causes of the First World War.

### Guidelines for the Online Discussion

1. **Respectful Language:** Always use polite and respectful language. Personal attacks, offensive comments, or derogatory language are strictly prohibited.

2. **Evidence-Based Discussion:** Support your arguments with evidence from credible sources. Cite your sources properly.

3. **Stay on Topic:** Keep the discussion focused on the topic of the First World War. Avoid deviating into unrelated subjects.

4. **Listen and Respond Thoughtfully:** Read others' posts carefully before responding. Aim to contribute new insights or questions that further the discussion.

5. **No Plagiarism:** Present your own ideas and when using someone else's work, give them credit.

6. **Confidentiality:** Keep discussions within the confines of the classroom. Do not share personal information or the contents of the discussion board outside of class.

7. **Regular Participation:** Try to participate regularly but avoid dominating the conversation. Give others a chance to express their views.

8. **Use of Multimedia:** Feel free to use images, videos, and links to articles as long as they are relevant to the topic and appropriate for a school setting.

9. **Be Open-Minded:** Be open to different perspectives and ready to learn something new.

10. **Netiquette:** Follow general internet etiquette rules. This includes not typing in all caps, which is considered shouting.

**Discussion Prompts**

1. **Prompt 1: Alliance Systems**—"Discuss how the complex system of alliances contributed to the outbreak of World War I. Were these alliances more defensive or aggressive in nature?"

2. **Prompt 2: The Role of Nationalism**—"Analyze the role of nationalism in precipitating World War I. Consider different nations and how nationalism manifested in each."

3. **Prompt 3: The Assassination of Archduke Franz Ferdinand**—"Evaluate the immediate and long-term impacts of Archduke Franz Ferdinand's assassination on the onset of World War I. Was this event the cause or just a catalyst?"

These guidelines and prompts should help create a meaningful and educational discussion about the First World War. Encourage your students to delve into each topic, bringing unique perspectives and historical insights to the table.

Looking at the list of guidelines that the chatbot generated, I would pick out the rules that fit the culture of my classroom and consider omitting the ones that don't. For example, I would exclude option 8 and instead encourage my students to use only text in their responses. You might want to tweak other guidelines before using them.

As for the discussion prompts, these are great conversation starters that require students to show solid understanding of the ideas that we have been learning about. You might decide to use only one question at a time to focus student attention and thinking on one concept while they also respond to what others have submitted in the discussion.

## Change It Up

How might we make changes to the original prompt to make it more useful for different learning situations? For one, we can create differentiated prompts so that all students are challenged at an appropriate level for the language skills:

> I want my tenth-grade students to use an online discussion board to learn more about the causes of the First World War. Create a prompt to start it. Create three versions of the prompt for students who are multilingual learners, those who are at-grade-level learners, and those with advanced skills.

### Sample Output

Discussion Prompts

For Multilingual Learners

- **Prompt:** "The First World War started in 1914. What do you think were the main reasons for this war? You can talk about countries, leaders, or big problems (like alliances or nationalism). Please use simple sentences and share one idea."

For At-Grade-Level Learners

- **Prompt:** "Consider the complex causes of World War I, including militarism, alliances, imperialism, and nationalism. Select one of these causes and explain how it contributed to the start of the war. Provide specific examples or events that illustrate your point."

For Advanced Learners

- **Prompt:** "Analyze the intricate web of causes leading to the outbreak of World War I, delving into the nuanced interplay of political, economic, and cultural factors. Argue for the primacy of one cause over others, using detailed historical evidence and considering counterarguments to your position. Your response should demonstrate a deep understanding of the era's geopolitical dynamics."

These prompts are designed to cater to the different language proficiencies and analytical skills of your students, encouraging each group to engage with the topic at an appropriate level.

The three prompts are closely related. Students are demonstrating their understanding of the historical events, but the prompts have customized instructions that ensure that all students are pushed to think deeply while respecting their different language skills.

If you don't know how discussions might work with your curriculum, why not ask the AI to help you brainstorm some ideas?

> ✦ I want my fifth-grade students to use an online discussion board in my family and consumer sciences class. What are some topics and discussion prompts that I could use?

## Try It Yourself

Even if you have never used discussions in your class, consider how this method might make them easier to implement. Using your knowledge of your curriculum (and perhaps a little help from the chatbot), write down some topics that might work well as discussions.

-------------------------------------------------------------------------

-------------------------------------------------------------------------

-------------------------------------------------------------------------

-------------------------------------------------------------------------

-------------------------------------------------------------------------

-------------------------------------------------------------------------

# Connecting the Dots: Show Relationships Between Concepts With Mind Mapping

*Mind mapping*, also known as concept mapping, is the visual organization of concepts (and sometimes subconcepts) to show interconnections. It is a powerful method that encourages students to reinforce their learning by illustrating the ways that different topics relate to one another. It requires summarization, as students choose individual terms and short descriptions to represent larger bits of text or notes. Mind mapping also stimulates students' creativity and makes them more active learners as they find different ways to arrange the ideas within a larger topic (Davies, 2011).

While it's not a new strategy—mind mapping was pioneered by author and education consultant Tony Buzan (2018) in the 1970s—many teachers don't feel comfortable using it with students or don't recognize its potential impact. Often, students have never been explicitly instructed in how to create a mind map. In other cases, students may think that they lack the creative ability to successfully make one. In my own experience, the key is to show students how mind maps work and provide examples as you build one together with them. Then, encourage students to use them as note-taking and review tools. Chatbots can help with each of those tasks:

> ✦ Create an explainer that describes what mind maps are and why they are so useful and that has instructions and tips for making one. Be sure that the text is appropriate for fifth graders.

### Sample Output

Absolutely! Here's an explainer about mind maps, tailored for fifth graders:

**What Are Mind Maps?**

Mind maps are like super-cool treasure maps for your brain! Imagine a big, colorful tree in the center of a paper. That's the main idea or topic you're thinking about. From this tree, branches grow out in all directions. These branches are smaller ideas or facts related to the main idea. Just like a tree has leaves, the branches of your mind map can have pictures, words, or even more tiny branches!

**Why Are Mind Maps Awesome?**

1. **Super Study Buddies:** Mind maps can turn boring notes into fun, easy-to-remember pictures. This makes studying for tests or remembering facts as easy as recalling a colorful image!

2. **Idea Factories:** They help you come up with new ideas! When you see how different thoughts connect, it's like a lightbulb turning on in your head.

3. **Organize Like a Pro:** Mind maps help you put your thoughts in order. It's like cleaning your room so you know where everything is.

**How to Make a Mind Map**

1. **Start With the Main Idea:** In the middle of a paper, write down your main idea or topic. Draw a big circle around it.

2. **Add Branches for Major Ideas:** Think of major ideas or subjects related to your main idea. Draw lines from your central idea to these "branches."

3. **Get Creative With Sub-Branches:** Add smaller lines from your major branches for more details. Like how a tree has smaller branches coming off the bigger ones.

4. **Color and Pictures:** Make your mind map colorful! Use different colors for different ideas. Draw pictures to help you remember things better.

5. **Keep It Simple:** Don't write long sentences. Use keywords or small phrases.

**Tips for an Awesome Mind Map**

- **Use Bright Colors:** Bright colors are not just fun, they help you remember things better.

- **Draw, Don't Worry About Art Skills:** Your drawings don't have to be perfect. They just need to help you remember your ideas.

- **Have Fun:** The more fun you have creating your mind map, the easier it will be to remember what's on it.

- **Share With Friends:** Sometimes, explaining your mind map to a friend can help you understand your topic even better.

Remember, your mind map is your brain on paper. There are no rules—just be creative and have fun! 🪄

I appreciate how approachable the description is and the way it clearly explains (without too much text) how to create a mind map. You could simply copy and paste this text into a document or online assignment to share with students. How else could we use the AI chatbot to help our students mind map?

## Change It Up

As I mentioned, one of the best ways to help students understand what a mind map looks like is to provide examples:

> ✦ Create a simple mind map using only text that shows how various kitchen tools are related to each other.

Here, I made sure to ask the chatbot for an example that is very different from what students will be asked to create so that they pay more attention to the structure than the actual content. Knowing that image-generating AI tools struggle quite a bit with text (see Explaining With Graphics in chapter 2, page 66), I intentionally requested a text-only mind map. This allows for the highest-quality output.

If you are looking to make the students' mind maps more useful for studying, you can also ask the chatbot to create reflection questions or quiz questions from a completed mind map by just uploading it with the prompt (for more examples of this, see Questioning the Image, page 82).

> ✦✦ A student created the attached mind map. What are some questions that they could consider or discuss to deepen their understanding of the connections presented in it? What quiz questions would check their understanding of it?

## Try It Yourself

Now, think about the topics that you teach and identify one or more that would be well suited to mind mapping. Choose one and use it with one of these prompts. List your favorite examples in the following space.

---------------------------------------------------------------

---------------------------------------------------------------

---------------------------------------------------------------

---------------------------------------------------------------

---------------------------------------------------------------

---------------------------------------------------------------

---------------------------------------------------------------

---------------------------------------------------------------

# Learning From Each Other: Maximize Collaborative Experiences for Students

Group work and collaboration have long been revered for the unique skills that they help students to develop. Now more than ever, these skills are critical for the careers of the 21st century. But there is a difference between simply requiring students to work in a group and using intentional lessons to foster and reinforce the habits that create successful collaborative learning experiences (Marzano, 2017; Marzano et al., 2001).

In many classrooms, including mine, teachers integrate collaborative skills with content lessons and activities throughout the school year. Students learn specific skills that help them be more cooperative, productive, and supportive of their teammates. To do this successfully, teachers need to identify ways that students can practice these skills within the learning experiences that they create. Teachers can easily turn some concepts into high-quality group work, but other curriculum standards don't seem to lend themselves as well to collaborative projects. As you have already seen, generative AI chatbots are very helpful in brainstorming ways to bridge that gap:

> **Create a collaborative group assignment for third-grade students who have just finished learning about place value in mathematics class. The lesson should include opportunities for students to learn cooperation, tolerance, and communication.**

## Sample Output

A collaborative group assignment for third-grade students who have just finished learning about place value could be both educational and engaging. Here's a suggestion for such an assignment:

**Assignment Title:** "Place Value Town Hall"

**Objective:** To reinforce the understanding of place value while fostering skills in cooperation, tolerance, and communication among third-grade students.

**Group Size:** four to five students per group

Materials Needed

- Large poster boards
- Markers, crayons, or colored pencils
- Sticky notes in various colors
- Place value charts and worksheets for reference
- Scissors and glue

Instructions

1. **Group Formation and Role Assignment** (ten minutes):
   - Divide the class into groups of four to five students.
   - In each group, assign roles like Mayor (leader), Architect (designer), Reporter (presenter), and Scribe (note-taker). Explain that each role is important and everyone must respect and listen to each other.

2. **Discussion and Planning** (fifteen minutes):
   - Each group discusses place value concepts and how they can represent these in a town layout.
   - Encourage students to share ideas and listen to each other, highlighting the importance of tolerance and cooperation.

3. **Creating Place Value Town** (thirty minutes):
   - Students design a town on their poster board where different buildings represent different place values (for example, "ones" could be houses, "tens" could be apartment buildings, "hundreds" could be large public buildings like libraries).
   - Each group member contributes to the drawing and construction, using their role to guide their participation.

4. **Labeling and Explanation** (fifteen minutes):
   - Use sticky notes to label the place values on each building.
   - The Scribe writes a brief explanation of the town's layout concerning place value.

5. **Presentation and Q&A Session** (twenty minutes):
   - Each group presents their Place Value Town to the class.
   - After the presentation, other students can ask questions. The group should work together to answer, showcasing their communication skills.

6. **Reflection and Group Dynamics Discussion** (ten minutes):
   - Students reflect on what they learned about place value.
   - The class discusses the group dynamics, focusing on how they communicated, cooperated, and showed tolerance toward different ideas.

7. **Assessment:**
   - Evaluate the groups on their understanding and representation of place values.
   - Observe and note the dynamics within the groups, focusing on cooperation, communication, and tolerance.
   - Provide feedback on how well they worked together and respected each other's roles and ideas.

This assignment is designed to not only reinforce mathematical concepts but also to nurture essential social skills that are vital for collaborative work. It encourages active participation, respectful listening, and the sharing of ideas, which are foundational skills for effective teamwork.

Notice that this is more than just a group project. It includes the selection of different roles and opportunities for students to discuss and make decisions together. These are important elements of a collaborative assignment. In output like this, I look for whether the focus of the project aligns with my content learning targets as well as whether the teamwork components are deeply integrated to ensure that students need to find ways to work together to complete the project.

## Change It Up

So, how can we take this idea and make it even more useful? In my classroom, students get year-long practice with cooperation and choosing roles within a group. If you want to incorporate these skills more completely and holistically into your teaching, try asking the chatbot for help:

> ✦✦✦ You are an expert high school humanities teacher with many years of experience, whose students truly enjoy the class. Create a system of collaborative roles and activities that could be used throughout a school year to help students develop group-work skills.

In response to this prompt, the chatbot will create a systemic plan for students to work successfully in groups multiple times throughout the year. In this way, collaboration becomes part of your classroom culture.

If you are struggling with a particular group-work skill gap among your students, you can adjust this type of prompt to focus on one or two skills at a time. While this is less holistic, it does present you with the opportunity to reflect or debrief after each activity, ensuring that students are developing the skills you intend:

> ✦✦✦ Create a collaborative group assignment for eighth-grade students who have just finished learning about human body systems. The lesson should include opportunities for students to learn how to communicate in respectful ways with one another.

## Try It Yourself

Whether you are a seasoned group-work instructor or this is your first foray into building collaborative skills, AI tools can be very helpful in brainstorming ways to meld your content lessons with the group skills that students will need in life. Craft a prompt like the ones in this section that you might use with your students and record it in the following space.

---

---

---

---

---

# Explaining It to Me: Create Opportunities for Students to Explain Their Learning

Many books and research articles have made a strong case for providing students with opportunities to explain their thinking to reveal what is going on inside their minds and how well they are learning (Hattie, 2023; Ritchhart, Church, & Morrison, 2011). Understanding what students are thinking is key to identifying and addressing learning gaps as well as crafting lessons that meet the needs of a wide variety of students. It also provides a mechanism for students to process and organize new information, which can lead to deeper understanding.

One of the most efficient ways to discover what and how students are thinking about a topic is to create opportunities in which they explain their understanding. This can be in the form of a written explanation or an audio or video recording of the student discussing what they've learned or what they are having trouble with. There are many ways to capture this information quickly and easily so that you can use it to personalize learning:

> ✦✦ **What are five ways that I can get students to explain their learning in my second-grade language arts class?**

### Sample Output

Engaging second-grade students in explaining their learning in language arts can be both fun and effective. Here are five creative ways to encourage them.

1. **Storytelling Circles:** Organize storytelling circles where each student gets a chance to narrate a part of a story or an experience related to the lesson. This method not only enhances speaking skills but also encourages active listening and collaboration among students.

2. **Illustrated Journals:** Have students maintain an illustrated journal. After a lesson, they can draw a picture related to what they learned and write a few sentences explaining it. This method is particularly effective as it combines visual and linguistic learning, making it easier for young learners to express and retain information.

3. **Role-Playing Activities:** Create role-playing scenarios related to the lesson. For example, if the lesson is about a specific story, students can enact scenes from it. This active engagement helps them understand and explain the material in a more profound way.

4. **Peer Teaching:** Pair up students and let them teach each other a concept they have just learned. This peer teaching method can boost understanding and confidence in explaining their learning, as they might feel more comfortable communicating with a fellow student.

5. **Digital Storytelling:** Utilize simple digital tools to let students create a digital story or presentation about what they have learned. They can use images, voice recordings, and text to explain the lesson. This approach is particularly engaging in today's tech-savvy world and helps develop digital literacy skills along with language arts.

Remember, the key is to keep the activities age-appropriate and interactive, ensuring that the students are engaged and motivated to express their understanding in creative ways.

When I look at a list like this, I check how well each suggestion aligns with my curriculum and how feasible each is for my classroom and students. I consider what supplies and preparation each will require, as well as the amount of preteaching I might have to do. In this case, I would definitely consider implementing the journaling idea (option 2), and I can see the value in options 4 and 5. Remember to always review the output from a chatbot carefully, especially when brainstorming, to filter out the ideas that won't work for you and your students.

## Change It Up

When you pick the ideas that you think will work for your class, don't be afraid to modify the ideas directly or make some changes to the prompt and see how the output evolves. If you already have an idea, you can modify the prompt to provide some of the necessary student documents:

> **I want my second-grade language arts students to do some illustrated journaling while they read and listen to me read a fable. Create a document that includes journaling prompts and other elements that will visualize their thinking.**

From this prompt, the AI chatbot provided me with text that I can edit and paste into a document to make a journal for students. Since the chatbot that I used in this example is multimodal (generates text as well as images, sounds, and video), it also created an image for the cover of the journal.

If you're looking for something that can more seamlessly gather examples of student thinking, try this modification:

> **You are a highly effective and efficient seventh-grade social studies teacher who is very skilled at finding quick ways to reveal student thinking. Create a quick method for students to explain their thinking about different economic systems after we have studied it.**

### Sample Output

As a highly effective seventh-grade social studies teacher, it's important to devise methods that are engaging, educational, and efficient in revealing students' understanding of different economic systems. Here's a quick and interactive method you can use.

Economic Systems Quick Pitch

1. **Prompt Preparation:** Prepare a set of cards or slips of paper with different economic scenarios or problems that societies face (for example, how to distribute resources, how to respond to a natural disaster, how to manage unemployment).

2. **Random Selection:** Have each student draw a card randomly.

3. **Individual Thinking Time:** Give students five minutes to think about how the economic system they studied (capitalism, socialism, communism, and so on) would handle the scenario on their card.

4. **Quick Pitch Session:** Each student then gets one minute to present their thoughts to the class or a small group. They should explain how their assigned economic system would approach the problem and why.

5. **Reflection and Discussion:** After all the pitches, open a brief class discussion. Encourage students to compare the different approaches of economic systems and reflect on the strengths and weaknesses of each.

6. **Exit Ticket:** As a closing activity, ask students to write a short paragraph on which economic system they believe would best handle the scenario they received and why, based on what they learned.

This activity is time-efficient, promotes quick thinking, and requires students to apply their knowledge of economic systems to real-world problems. It also encourages public speaking and critical thinking skills.

Notice how the perspective priming (see Tips for Teams, page 90, in this chapter) helped focus the chatbot on my specific needs for this prompt. This helped me get just the output that I needed without as much back and forth in the conversation.

## Try It Yourself

Whether you already use strategies for revealing student thinking or this technique is new for you, generative AI models can help you brainstorm ideas that fit your classroom culture and curriculum and then help you build the resources that you will need to implement them. Think of a topic that you teach and test out some prompts like the ones in this section to get useful materials. Capture your best prompt example in the following space.

------------------------------------------------------------

------------------------------------------------------------

------------------------------------------------------------

------------------------------------------------------------

------------------------------------------------------------

------------------------------------------------------------

## Chapter Reflection

Teaching new content without spending time reinforcing student understanding is like trying to make bread without kneading the dough. Students need repeated exposure to new ideas and multiple opportunities to practice new skills before these will become integrated into the memory structures in their brains. This is a fundamental key to forming long-term memory that will help our students in later coursework.

More importantly, the more time and effort students put into grappling with new concepts, the deeper their understanding will be. This means that they will be able to draw connections with other topics and even other subjects. It also strengthens their critical-thinking skills to make them better learners overall. Such reinforcement doesn't happen by accident; teachers need to build these opportunities intentionally.

To that end, this chapter explores a variety of generative AI prompts to facilitate this work by looking at ways for students to practice new skills and knowledge (Questioning the Image, Doing the Math, and Giving Them Choice) and methods of building deeper understanding through interaction (Showing Me the Data, Talking About It, Learning From Each Other, Connecting the Dots, and Explaining It to Me). It also explores prompts that would make students more motivated (Answering "How Can I Use This?") and more able to recall what they've learned (Saying *Yes SIR*).

In the next chapter, we'll check out how chatbots can make assessment more powerful.

# Chapter 3 Questions for Discussion

What is a pain point for you and your students when it comes to reviewing and reinforcing learning? Which of these prompts has the most potential to improve the experience for you and for them?

How will the use of AI tools change the way you provide practice opportunities to your students?

What's your best technique for building deeper content understanding in your students? How might it be made more efficient with the help of AI?

# CHAPTER 4

# Assessing Student Mastery

As part of my own journey as an educator, I regularly ask my students what I'm doing well and what I can do better to help them learn science. The most common bit of positive feedback that I get from them is that I do a good job of treating assessments more as measurements than accomplishments. They enjoy the low-stakes, formative attitude that I try to infuse into our tests and quizzes. They do not, survey says, enjoy my dad jokes. That formative attitude extends into my frequent use of formative assessment in a variety of ways, such as informal questioning, exit tickets, think-pair-shares, and peer review. The work of many authors and researchers (Bailey & Jakicic, 2023; Marzano, Norford, & Ruyle, 2019; Wiliam, 2018) has shown the value of these practices for improving student engagement and learning.

A fundamental inflection point in any learning cycle occurs when we pause learning to determine how much progress students have made. This critical step forms a fork in the instructional road: Does the learner have sufficient mastery to move on to another topic? Or do we need more time and practice to get there? To serve this purpose, though, assessment must have the following attributes.

- **Valid:** It needs to measure what it sets out to measure and only that.
- **Reliable:** Results should be consistent and reproducible.
- **Fair:** All students should have an equitable assessment experience.
- **Clear:** Both teachers and students need to understand the format, objectives, and success criteria.
- **Practical:** The size of the assessment needs to be feasible for students to complete in a reasonable time and for teachers to grade it and offer feedback promptly.

With the enormous variety of assessment types available to them, teachers are faced with the challenge of choosing the best way to test their students given the specifics of their learning targets, classroom logistics, and technology resources. Whether they select a computerized format or a paper-and-pencil one often boils down to which one can be constructed and scored most easily. Good assessment takes time, but prompt feedback is also critical to the learning process (Ferriter & Cancellieri, 2017). However, making these important decisions gets a lot easier with the aid of AI. In this chapter, we explore ten prompts that produce a wide variety of useful assessments.

## Organizing and Studying: Build Interactive Study Guides

Before an official test or quiz, students benefit from working alone or in groups to complete a study guide. A study guide helps them organize their notes and ensure that they have all the necessary information. Interactive study guides include a variety of study exercises that challenge students to determine what they already have committed to memory and which topics need further review. The most effective study guides can also be the most time consuming for educators to create. Let's ask a chatbot to help:

> ✦✦ **Create an interactive study guide for tenth-grade students to review complex numbers.**

### Sample Output

Creating an interactive study guide for tenth-grade students to review complex numbers involves several key components to make it effective and engaging. Here's a structured approach to designing such a guide.

1. **Introduction to Complex Numbers**
   - **Definition:** Introduce the concept of complex numbers, explaining that they include a real part and an imaginary part.
   - **Historical Context:** Briefly mention the history and the reason for the development of complex numbers.

2. **Fundamental Concepts**
   - **Understanding $i$:** Explain the imaginary unit $i$, where ($i^2 = -1$).
   - **Form of Complex Numbers:** Demonstrate the standard form ($a + bi$), where $a$ and $b$ are real numbers.
   - **Real and Imaginary Parts:** Clarify how to identify the real part and the imaginary part of a complex number.

3. **Arithmetic With Complex Numbers**
   - **Addition and Subtraction:** Provide examples and practice problems.
   - **Multiplication:** Explain the process, including multiplying by $i$.
   - **Division:** Show how to divide complex numbers using conjugates.

4. **Graphical Representation**
   - **Complex Plane:** Introduce the concept of the complex plane, with real and imaginary axes.
   - **Plotting Complex Numbers:** Interactive exercises for plotting complex numbers.

5. **Advanced Concepts**
   - **Magnitude and Argument:** Explain how to find the magnitude and argument of a complex number.
   - **Euler's Formula:** Introduce Euler's formula as an advanced concept.

6. **Practical Applications**
   - **Real-World Applications:** Discuss how complex numbers are used in engineering, physics, and other fields.

7. **Interactive Components**
   - **Quizzes:** Include quizzes at the end of each section for self-assessment.
   - **Interactive Visualizations:** Use tools like GeoGebra for students to visualize complex numbers on the complex plane.
   - **Games and Puzzles:** Incorporate educational games to reinforce concepts.

8. **Additional Resources**
   - **Further Reading:** Suggest books and websites for more in-depth learning.
   - **Video Tutorials:** Provide links to educational videos for different learning styles.

9. **Summary and Review**
   - **Recap of Key Points:** Summarize the most important concepts.
   - **Final Assessment:** Offer a comprehensive test covering all topics.

10. **Feedback and Improvement**
    - **Feedback Form:** Include a form for students to provide feedback on the guide.
    - **Updates and Improvements:** Regularly update the guide based on feedback and new educational research.

**Technical Aspects**

- **Platform:** Decide whether the guide will be web-based, an app, or a downloadable PDF with interactive elements.
- **Accessibility:** Ensure the guide is accessible to students with different needs, including those with visual or auditory impairments.

This guide, designed with engaging content and interactive elements, can effectively help tenth-grade students in understanding and mastering complex numbers.

As you look over this sample output, you'll notice that it provides a detailed plan for what the study guide could be, but it doesn't actually create any of the components. In fact, it recommends several different options for the format (web-based, app, or PDF). This shortcoming is likely due to the AI model's inability to generate specific file types. For example, say we try to ask the chatbot to create two of the suggested components of the study guide:

> **Can you create the text for #1 and #2 above?**

## Sample Output

Certainly! Here's the text for sections 1 and 2 of the interactive study guide, focusing on the introduction and fundamental concepts of complex numbers:

1. **Introduction to Complex Numbers**

   Welcome to the World of Complex Numbers!

   Complex numbers are a fascinating and essential concept in mathematics, extending the idea of what numbers can be. Unlike the regular numbers we use in daily life, complex numbers include a real part and an imaginary part. This unique combination allows us to solve equations that were once thought impossible to solve!

   **A Brief History:** Complex numbers first appeared in the 16th century, thanks to the efforts of mathematicians like Gerolamo Cardano and Rafael Bombelli. They were exploring solutions to cubic equations and stumbled upon the square roots of negative numbers. Over time, these "impossible" numbers gained acceptance and became a crucial part of mathematics, especially in fields like engineering and physics.

2. **Fundamental Concepts of Complex Numbers**

   **What Is $i$ in Complex Numbers?** In complex numbers, $i$ represents the square root of $-1$. It's what we call an imaginary unit. This might sound strange at first because we are used to numbers having positive or negative square roots that are real numbers. But in the world of complex numbers, $i$ allows us to expand our understanding of what numbers can be. Remember: $[i^2 = -1]$

   **Standard Form of Complex Numbers:** A complex number is usually written in the form $(a + bi)$. Here, $a$ and $b$ are real numbers; $a$ is known as the real part, and $bi$ is the imaginary part. For example, in the complex number $3 + 4i$, 3 is the real part, and $4i$ is the imaginary part.

   **Identifying Real and Imaginary Parts:** To identify the real and imaginary parts of a complex number, just look at the number's structure. The real part is the number without the *i*, and the imaginary part is the number with the *i*. For instance, in 5 – 2*i*, the real part is 5, and the imaginary part is –2*i*.

This text provides a concise yet thorough introduction to complex numbers, setting the stage for more advanced topics. The language and examples are tailored to be accessible to tenth-grade students, ensuring they can grasp these foundational concepts before moving on to more complex material.

Here, the AI produced text that I can copy, paste in a blank document or web page, and tweak to create those sections of the study guide. This gives teachers the freedom to choose the format that works best for them (for example, a Google Sites website with multiple linked pages) and populate the study guide with the generative AI text that has been edited for clarity and accuracy.

## Change It Up

If you're looking for a more concise tool to organize review material for students, you can adjust the prompt to produce something smaller:

> ✦ Create a one-page study guide for tenth-grade students to study complex numbers. Provide the students with ideas for studying. Rather than an outline, give me the actual text of the study guide.

Notice that, to save a step, I prompted the AI to both design and build the study guide. For smaller documents, this takes you straight to the editing step so that you can make use of the resources more quickly.

If you're looking to differentiate better for the range of mastery levels in your classroom, you can prompt the chatbot to generate levels of study guide. Then, assign them to your students based on classroom data (see Getting Them Warmed Up, Capturing Quick Data, and Checking Out, starting on page 116).

> ✦ Create a one-page study guide for fifth-grade students to study geography. Create a version for students who are struggling to understand the concepts, one for students who have a basic grasp of the concepts, and one for students who have a more advanced understanding of the concepts. Rather than an outline, give me the actual text of the study guides.

## Try It Yourself

Choose a topic that you teach and explore the types of study guides that an AI chatbot can create. Were there any activities that were new to you, or that you have been looking to add to your teaching toolbox? Capture the ones that show promise in the following space.

--------------------------------------------------------------------------------

--------------------------------------------------------------------------------

--------------------------------------------------------------------------------

--------------------------------------------------------------------------------

--------------------------------------------------------------------------------

--------------------------------------------------------------------------------

--------------------------------------------------------------------------------

# Getting Them Warmed Up: Craft Useful and Engaging Daily Warm-Up Exercises

Warm-up activities, also called do-nows, starters, bell-ringers, or walk-ins, are often writing prompts, review questions, or prediction activities that students are assigned to complete when they first arrive to class. They offer many benefits to students and the learning atmosphere of a classroom (Marzano, 2017; Marzano et al., 2001).

- Building a sense of community by having students participate in a classroom routine
- Acting as icebreakers to reduce student reluctance to participate in class
- Creating a clear transition from the previous class to the current one
- Allowing time for administrative tasks like taking attendance

In my classroom, the primary role of warm-ups is to measure student mastery before a lesson begins. Approximately half the time, I ask questions that gauge how well my students have mastered the lesson from the previous day. I can use this information to adjust my plan for the current day, correcting misconceptions and closing learning gaps. The other half of the time, my warm-up questions offer a preview of the day's lesson. Student responses to this type of question also help me plan for the day by revealing what preexisting knowledge some of my students have, giving me an opportunity to personalize the lesson for their needs.

Sometimes it can be challenging to craft just the right warm-up activity. Ideally, these exercises will be engaging to students so that you don't need to push them to complete the warm-up every day. They will also provide quick data that you can use right away as part of your lesson for the day. It's also a great idea to mix them up and include enough variety that they don't get boring for you or your students. A generative AI tool is the ideal way to brainstorm some ideas:

> ✦✦ **Give me five possible warm-up questions that can be used at the start of a third-grade class about the planets of our solar system. Provide a variety of formats and difficulty levels. Make the questions engaging for students and easy to analyze by the teacher.**

### Sample Output

Certainly! Here are five engaging warm-up questions about the planets of our solar system, suitable for a third-grade class. These questions vary in format and difficulty, aiming to capture the students' interest and facilitate easy analysis for the teacher.

1. **Multiple Choice:** "Which planet is known as the Red Planet?"

    a. Venus

    b. Mars

    c. Jupiter

    d. Saturn

2. **True or False:** "Saturn is the only planet in our solar system with rings."

    True

    False

3. **Fill in the Blank:** "_____ is the largest planet in our solar system."

4. **Short Answer:** "What makes Earth different from all the other planets in our solar system?"

5. **Drawing Activity:** "Draw and label two planets of your choice, and write one interesting fact about each."

These questions cover a range of topics within the theme of planets and are designed to be both educational and enjoyable for young learners.

Looking at the output from the prompt, I like that the chatbot provided a wide range of different types of questions. This gives you a chance to choose the type that works best for your classroom situation or the information that you need. If you find a type that you like, you can ask the chatbot to generate variations on that one. Or, consider a regular pattern of warm-ups, such as True–False Tuesday and Write-About-It Wednesday, to keep things interesting while maintaining routines.

## Change It Up

If you're looking for more open-ended responses to gain better insight into students' thinking, you can modify the prompt to focus on just that type of warm-up question:

> ✦ Give me five possible warm-up questions that can be used at the start of a third-grade class about the planets of our solar system. All the questions should be open ended and able to be completed in about five minutes.

Or, if your goal is to prime your students for the day's lesson, try asking them to predict the focus of the lesson given some key vocabulary:

> ✦ My fifth-grade students are getting ready to learn about the order of the planets in the solar system. Create a warm-up question that prompts them to predict the topic of today's class using several key vocabulary words as clues.

## Try It Yourself

Whether you prefer quick multiple-choice questions or more open-ended ones to kick off a class period, you should find some potential in this prompt. Try the original prompt or one of the suggested modifications and use the following space to consider how the output might change your classroom routine.

# Capturing Quick Data: Make Options for Short, Useful Assessments

The key to powerful assessment habits in your classroom is just that: making it a habit. When small, low-stakes assessments are given frequently, students become less anxious about them. When we review the data from these assessments with them, they begin to see their value. In my experience, students are less likely to cheat when we act on the data and use them as a lever for growth. Research has found that assessments linked with more frequent feedback have the biggest impact on learning (Hattie, 2023).

While simple, informal questioning of students is often the best way to discover what your students know, it is also very inefficient. A good low-stakes assessment strategy will include conversations with students combined with short, easily scored data-capture tools. These assessments will provide data that you can use to change the direction or pace of a lesson on the fly or to shift the plan for the upcoming days:

> ✦˙ ✦ **What are three options for gathering quick assessment data in the middle of my seventh-grade language arts class?**

### Sample Output

Gathering quick assessment data in the middle of a seventh-grade language arts class is a great way to gauge student understanding in real time and adjust your teaching as needed. Here are three effective options.

1. **Think-Pair-Share:** This activity involves students first thinking individually about a question or topic, then discussing their thoughts with a partner, and finally sharing with the larger class. This method provides immediate insight into student understanding and allows for peer learning. It's especially useful for assessing comprehension of a reading passage or discussion topic.

2. **Polling or Clicker Systems:** Use technology like polling software (for example, Poll Everywhere) or clicker systems to ask quick, formative questions during the lesson. Students can respond via devices, and you get instant feedback on their understanding. This is particularly effective for multiple-choice or true–false questions and can quickly highlight concepts that need more clarification.

3. **Whiteboard Responses:** Distribute mini-whiteboards to each student or pair of students. Throughout the lesson, pose questions and have students write their responses on the whiteboards and show them. This method provides a visual and immediate gauge of student understanding and can cover a range of question types, from short answers to solving language-related problems.

Each of these strategies is interactive and engages students actively in the learning process. They also allow for immediate adjustment in teaching strategies based on the real-time data gathered about student understanding.

This is a great example of the power of generative AI tools to augment the work of a teacher. You may already have one or more of these examples in your toolbox of classroom strategies, but it can be difficult to remember all of them in a moment when you need to choose one. And it can be especially challenging to select one that matches the needs of the lesson. By asking your AI assistant to provide a handful of ideas, you can make smarter choices to get the quick data that you need.

Reflecting on the sample output from this prompt, I recognize that the second idea might involve quite a bit of preparation on the part of students and teacher alike. My students enjoy think-pair-share opportunities, though, and I can initiate one quickly without needing to explain the protocol. The mini-whiteboard idea is not one that I regularly use, but I think it would be a great way to gather some fast data and get students actively grappling with the content that we are learning, especially if you already have a set of these whiteboards or a similar way to get students responding.

## Change It Up

Once you have one or more strategies in mind, why not modify the prompt to give you specific ideas for that protocol?

> ✦✦ **My seventh-grade language arts students just learned about tone. What are four think-pair-share prompts that I could give them?**

### Sample Output

That's a great way to engage your students in understanding and applying their knowledge of tone in language arts. Here are four think-pair-share prompts that could be effective.

1. **Identifying Tone in Literature:** Ask the students to think of a favorite book or story and identify the overall tone of the work. They should consider how the author's choice of words and style contribute to this tone. After they've had a moment to think, they can pair up and share their examples, discussing how the tone affects their perception of the story.

2. **Tone in Everyday Communication:** Prompt the students to recall a recent conversation they had (with a friend, family member, or teacher) and analyze the tone used. Was it formal, informal, friendly, hostile, or something else? They should think about how the tone influenced the direction and outcome of the conversation. In pairs, they can share their insights and discuss how tone plays a role in everyday communication.

3. **Creating Tone Through Writing:** Challenge the students to write a short paragraph about a neutral topic (like describing a room or a weather condition). The twist is they should write it twice, each time with a different tone (for example, cheerful versus gloomy, calm versus anxious). After writing, they can pair up to share their paragraphs and discuss how their word choices and sentence structures created different tones.

4. **Tone in Media:** Ask students to think about a TV show, movie, or song they recently enjoyed. What was the tone of that media piece? How did the creators convey this tone through visuals, dialogue, music, and so on? After reflecting, students can pair up and share their examples, discussing how tone contributes to the overall impact of media on its audience.

These prompts encourage students to think critically about tone in various contexts and share their insights with peers, fostering a deeper understanding of the concept.

Remember to always ask for several prompts or examples so that you can choose the one that will work best for your specific situation. This is the key to the teacher-AI partnership.

## Try It Yourself

Now put this idea to the test by creating one or more quick in-class assessments that will reveal your students' mastery of whatever you are teaching. Record the best examples in the following space.

---

---

---

---

---

---

---

---

# Checking Out: Use Exit Tickets Effectively

Exit tickets are another great example of a simple, quick, low-stakes assessment that can give you the information that you need to plan your lessons and differentiate in meaningful ways (Meer & Chapman, 2014). By definition, teachers usually give them at the end of class, and, often, submitting one's finished exit ticket is required before leaving class. I love to use exit tickets in my class because I have time to look over the responses before the next class, and our frequent use of them has turned them into a low-pressure routine for my students.

Crafting exit tickets can be a challenging task. They need to be quick for students to complete but also fast for teachers to analyze. They must measure the critical skills of the completed lesson while also capturing student misconceptions. The ideal exit ticket will be a small piece of paper or brief digital questionnaire that can be sorted by the teacher to get an overall sense of mastery while also allowing for skill-level grouping. Let's give it a try:

> I am teaching my third-grade students about rounding numbers to the nearest 10 or 100. I need four ideas for quick exit ticket assessments that could be given at the end of the lesson.

### Sample Output

Exit ticket assessments are a great way to quickly gauge your third graders' understanding of rounding numbers to the nearest 10 or 100. Here are four ideas you can use.

1. **Quick Oral Quiz:** Ask each student a rounding question as they line up at the door to leave. For example, "Round 235 to the nearest 10" or "What is 480 rounded to the nearest 100?"

2. **Estimation Challenge:** Present a number and ask students to quickly write down both the nearest 10 and nearest 100 on a slip of paper. This not only tests their rounding skills but also their ability to quickly estimate.

3. **Matching Game:** Provide cards with numbers on one set and their rounded counterparts on another. Students must match each number to its rounded value.

4. **Reflective Questionnaire:** Ask students to write a short reflection on what they learned about rounding, including an example of a number they rounded and how they did it.

Remember, the key is to keep the assessments quick yet effective in evaluating their understanding of the rounding concept.

I think that most teachers would have no trouble choosing one of these various suggestions that works for them (and if not, don't forget you can run the prompt again or ask for more options at a time). For example, I know that the estimation challenge (option 2) would be a great exit ticket for my students. But I don't think that an oral option (like option 1) would work because they would stress out about the pressure of it. The reflective questionnaire (option 4) seems like it would take my students too long to complete, but I think the matching game (option 3) would be a quick option, and I could make a set of cards for each group of students with slightly different numbers to ensure that the data I collect are more accurate than if students copy responses from one another.

## Change It Up

As we've seen before, if you find a type of exit ticket that you like, it's easy to ask the chatbot to create the actual assessment for you. You can even ask it to create multiple versions so that you can minimize cheating:

> ✦✦  I am teaching my third-grade students about rounding numbers to
> the nearest 10 or 100. Make me a quick number line exercise that
> could be an exit ticket. Make four versions of the exercise at the
> same difficulty level.

> ✦✦  I am teaching my third-grade students about rounding numbers
> to the nearest 10 or 100. Make me a quick worksheet that could
> be used as an exit ticket. It should fill no more than half of a page.
> Make five versions at the same difficulty level.

Or, if you have an idea of what might be the biggest stumbling block for your students, try asking the chatbot to make an exit ticket that focuses on measuring mastery of one critical skill:

> ✦✦  I am teaching my third-grade students about rounding numbers to
> the nearest 10 or 100. Make me a quick exit ticket worksheet that
> measures their ability to round when the final digit is a 5. It should
> fill no more than half of a page. Make five versions at the same
> difficulty level.

## Try It Yourself

Whether you use exit tickets in your class every day already or are looking for ways to start incorporating them into a new assessment routine, these sample prompts provide the kickstart that you'll need to get generative AI tools to help you. Try one out and record your observations in the following space.

# Looking in the Mirror: Generate Tools for Student Self-Assessment

The ultimate goal of any educational program is to help our students develop the skills to become independent lifelong learners. One of the most critical skills needed for this development is the ability to assess one's own learning and make changes to improve it (McMillan & Hearn, 2008). Most K–12 students need explicit instruction to help them learn to do this, and that means that we have a mandate to teach our students how to self-assess.

Creating opportunities for student self-assessment can seem like a mammoth task for educators. How do we choose the right ways to teach these skills? How do we provide students with the best types of practice? Can we assess their ability to self-assess? Let's work with an AI chatbot to find the answers:

> ✦ **How can a sixth-grade teacher begin to teach their students how to self-assess their learning?**

### Sample Output

Teaching sixth-grade students to self-assess their learning is a valuable skill that promotes metacognition and a deeper understanding of their own learning process. Here are some strategies a sixth-grade teacher can employ to introduce and support self-assessment.

1. **Introduce the Concept of Self-Assessment:** Start by explaining what self-assessment is and why it's important. Discuss how it helps students understand their strengths and areas for improvement, and how it can make them more independent learners.

2. **Use Simple Self-Assessment Tools:** Start with basic tools like checklists or smiley face scales where students can easily indicate their understanding of a topic. These tools should be straightforward and age-appropriate.

3. **Model Self-Assessment:** Demonstrate how to self-assess by using examples. Show students how to reflect on their work, identify their strengths, and recognize areas where they need more practice or support.

4. **Set Clear Learning Goals and Criteria:** Help students understand what they are learning and why. Clearly define the learning objectives and criteria for success. This can be in the form of rubrics or simple goal statements.

5. **Incorporate Peer Assessment:** Allow students to assess each other's work. This not only provides additional perspectives but also helps them understand the assessment criteria better.

By gradually incorporating these strategies, a 6th-grade teacher can effectively teach their students to self-assess, fostering greater independence and a deeper understanding of their own learning process.

This example is edited down—the original answer gave ten options, but this excerpt gives you an idea of the comprehensiveness the AI can achieve. You might find that you don't have the time or the resources for all the steps it can give you. Or, your students may already have some of these skills, and you may jump into this sequence in a later phase. It also looks like this plan would take the better part of an entire school year to complete. If you're looking for resources on a smaller scale, you can make some changes to the prompt. For more details about peer assessment (option 5), see Correcting One Another (later in this chapter, page 132).

## Change It Up

One simple change that you can make to the original prompt is to focus on one specific skill at a time, and ask the chatbot to create a variety of sample resources:

> What are some simple checklists and other beginning self-assessment tools that a sixth grader can use?

> What are some journaling prompts that a sixth-grade teacher could use to help students begin to learn self-assessment?

> I am a sixth-grade teacher with students who are becoming skilled at self-assessment. What are some ways that I can assess their self-assessment skills?

Each of these will generate ideas and resources for one of the stages in the process of learning. See how you can get as specific as you need to in the prompt while still asking for several results so that you can choose the best?

## Try It Yourself

Consider how you use self-assessment in your classroom right now and how you would like to in the future. How do you plan to use these prompts? Record your ideas in the following space.

-------------------------------------------------------------------

-------------------------------------------------------------------

-------------------------------------------------------------------

-------------------------------------------------------------------

-------------------------------------------------------------------

## Setting Clear Expectations: Generate Useful Rubrics for Equitable Grading

Open-ended assessments, such as essays, projects, and labs, provide unmatched authentic student mastery data, but they also introduce significant obstacles to fair grading (Stallings-Roberts, 1992; Wormeli, 2024). Any question that includes subjectivity in its grading should spark discussion among the team of teachers who will grade it. The best response is the creation of a grading rubric for scoring this type of question (Guskey & Brookhart, 2019). This process can be time consuming, though, and several online products, including iRubric (www.rcampus.com/indexrubric.cfm) and RubiStar (http://rubistar.4teachers.org/index.php), sprouted up in the early 2000s, before AI gained traction, to address this challenge. Given the power of rubrics and their need to be customized to each assignment, AI tools seem an obvious pick to support teachers in this work. They can create ready-to-use customized rubrics very quickly that your team can use to ensure that all student responses are graded consistently and fairly:

> Create a rubric that could be used to score the answers to this question for a group of eighth graders: What is the most important way that humans can be good stewards of Earth's water resources? Be sure to score students based on their answer's accuracy, creativity, and completeness. The total number of points available for this question is 30.

### Sample Output

Here's a rubric designed for scoring the answers of eighth graders to the question, What is the most important way that humans can be good stewards of Earth's water resources? The rubric is divided into three main criteria: Accuracy, Creativity, and Completeness. Each criterion has a maximum score, contributing to a total of 30 points.

**Rubric for Water Stewardship Question (Total Points: 30)**

1. **Accuracy (10 Points)**

   - **0–3 Points:** The answer shows minimal or no understanding of water stewardship. It contains significant inaccuracies.

   - **4–6 Points:** The answer demonstrates a basic understanding of water stewardship but includes some inaccuracies or misconceptions.

   - **7–8 Points:** The answer is mostly accurate and demonstrates a good understanding of water stewardship.

   - **9–10 Points:** The answer is highly accurate, showing an excellent understanding of water stewardship concepts and practices.

2. **Creativity (10 Points)**

   - **0–3 Points:** The answer lacks originality, simply restates common ideas, and shows little creative thinking.

- **4–6 Points:** The answer shows some originality and creative thinking but remains largely conventional.
- **7–8 Points:** The answer is creative, presenting unique or insightful ideas or perspectives on water stewardship.
- **9–10 Points:** The answer is exceptionally creative, offering innovative and thoughtful ideas that demonstrate deep engagement with the topic.

3. **Completeness (10 Points)**

- **0–3 Points:** The answer is incomplete, missing key aspects or details regarding water stewardship.
- **4–6 Points:** The answer is somewhat complete but lacks certain details or depth in discussing water stewardship.
- **7–8 Points:** The answer is complete, covering the main aspects of water stewardship with adequate detail.
- **9–10 Points:** The answer is exceptionally complete, thoroughly and comprehensively covering water stewardship in detail.

**Note:** Teachers should encourage students to provide examples, reasoning, and elaborate on their ideas wherever possible. The rubric aims to assess not just factual knowledge, but also the students' ability to think critically and creatively about environmental stewardship.

The bits of editorial content that the chatbot provides at the beginning and end of its responses can be helpful. Often, they can act as gentle reminders of best practices for educators. The rubric itself provides great guidance for the teachers who will be grading responses, and, with some light editing, this text could also be useful guidance to students as they craft their answers. Let's look at some ways to make this type of rubric even more useful for specific situations.

## Change It Up

If you prefer to get the rubric in a grid format for easier grading, the chatbot can do that with ease:

> Create a rubric that could be used to score the answers to this question for a group of eighth graders: What is the most important way that humans can be good stewards of Earth's water resources? Be sure to score students based on their answer's accuracy, creativity, and completeness. The total number of points available for this question is 30. Provide the rubric in a grid format.

Or, if you are not sure what categories should be in the rubric, the AI can provide options:

> ✦✦ My ninth-grade students are going to be answering an essay question
> about art movements of the 19th century. What are ten different
> categories that I should have in the grading rubric for this question?

If you are working to emphasize self-assessment (see Looking in the Mirror, page 124), why not create a version of the rubric that students can use for that purpose before submitting it to you?

> ✦✦ Create a rubric that could be used by eighth-grade students to
> score their answers to this question: What is the most important
> way that humans can be good stewards of Earth's water resources?
> Help students score their answer's accuracy, creativity, and
> completeness and phrase the descriptors as questions that
> students can ask themselves.

Rubrics can be very powerful tools that are an important part of the assessment process and the development of a healthy classroom culture around grading. We can and should be using them more often in our work. And generative AI tools can make them more feasible.

## Try It Yourself

Think of an open-ended assessment that you plan to use (or have used in the past) and use one of the prompt ideas in this section to generate a grading rubric for it. What did the chatbot get right? Where did it fall short? Record your reflections in the following space.

----------

----------

----------

----------

----------

----------

----------

# Showing What It Should Look Like: Create Exemplars to Demonstrate What You Expect

Education research has shown repeatedly that students are more able to meet expectations and do so with more confidence when they are presented with examples of what a teacher expects finished work to look like (Hendry, Armstrong, & Bromberger, 2012; Smyth & Carless, 2021). More than just clarifying expectations, these exemplars serve to inspire students and reduce anxiety about the expected level of mastery. High-level examples can give students a goal to reach for, and low-level ones can provide a warning about common missteps. It should come as no surprise that generative AI models are great at generating exemplars for just about any task:

> ✦✦ **My fourth-grade students are writing a letter to their state legislative representative persuading them to support a four-day school week. Provide an exemplar that shows what an excellent letter would look like.**

### Sample Output

Certainly! Here's an example of a persuasive letter that a fourth-grade student might write to their state legislative representative advocating for a four-day school week:

**[Student's Name]**
**[School Name]**
**[School Address]**
**[City, State, Zip Code]**

**[Date]**

**[Representative's Name]**
**[Office Address]**
**[City, State, Zip Code]**

Dear [Representative's Name],

I hope this letter finds you well. My name is [Student's Name], and I am a fourth grader at [School Name] in [City]. I am writing to you to discuss something important to me and my classmates: the possibility of having a four-day school week in our state.

I understand that the idea of a shorter school week might seem unusual at first, but there are many reasons why this could be beneficial for students, teachers, and even the environment. Here are a few points I would like you to consider.

1. **Improved Mental Health:** A four-day school week could give students more time to rest and engage in activities they enjoy, leading to better mental health and well-being. This extra day off could help reduce stress and anxiety, which is something many of us experience.

2. **More Family Time:** A three-day weekend would mean more quality time with our families. This is especially important for families where parents work long hours during the week. We would cherish this extra day to bond and make memories together.

3. **Environmental Impact:** Fewer school days mean less commuting. This could reduce carbon emissions from school buses and parents' cars, contributing to a healthier planet. It's a small change, but every bit helps when it comes to protecting our environment.

4. **Enhanced Focus in School:** With a longer weekend to recharge, students might be more focused and productive during the four days we are in school. This could lead to better academic performance and a more positive attitude toward learning.

I understand that there are challenges to consider, such as childcare for parents who work five days a week and ensuring that we still receive a high-quality education. However, I believe that with careful planning and open-mindedness, these challenges can be overcome.

I am passionate about this idea because I truly believe it could make a positive difference in the lives of students, teachers, and our community. I hope you will consider the potential benefits of a four-day school week and support this change in our education system.

Thank you for taking the time to read my letter. I look forward to your response and any thoughts you might have on this matter.

Sincerely,

[Student's Name]

This letter serves as an exemplar by being well-structured, respectful, and providing clear, thoughtful arguments. It's important for the students to personalize their letters with their own thoughts and experiences.

This sample letter does a good job of representing the ideal student work sample. However, sometimes that is not the best tool for guiding students. In my classroom, students who see a perfect exemplar like this will be tempted to mimic it so closely that I will end up receiving a dozen or more submissions that are nearly exact copies of it. So, how do we change this prompt to support students while also encouraging them to be more creative?

## Change It Up

One of the best ways that I have found to clarify expectations without providing students with a strict path to follow is by giving them poor-quality exemplars. I show students what a D- or C-level submission looks like, and then they need to figure out what it's lacking as they create their own work:

> ✦✦ **My fourth-grade students are writing a letter to their state legislative representative persuading them to support a four-day school week. Provide an exemplar that shows what a subpar letter would look like.**

### Sample Output

Dear [Representative's Name],

I think school should be four days a week. This is a good idea because we will have more time to play and do stuff we like. School is sometimes boring and hard, and we need more breaks. Also, if we have a four-day week, we can sleep more.

I hope you like my idea. Please make school four days a week. Thanks.

Sincerely,

[Student's Name]

---

**Key Areas for Improvement**

1. **Lack of structure:** The letter doesn't have a clear introduction, body, and conclusion.

2. **Weak arguments:** The reasons provided are vague and not compelling. They focus on personal desires rather than broader benefits.

3. **Formal tone:** The tone is too informal for a letter to a legislative representative.

4. **Details and evidence:** There are no specific examples or evidence to support the claims.

5. **Grammar and spelling:** While not overly poor, the language could be more polished to appear professional and respectful.

By analyzing this subpar letter, your students can learn how to avoid these mistakes and write a more persuasive and well-structured letter.

This output includes not only the exemplar text but also a short list of the reasons why it would earn a lower score. Providing the explanation alongside the exemplar to students will help them better understand the expectations of the assignment.

Alternatively, I also like to provide students with exemplars that demonstrate the right format and rigor but center on a similar writing prompt. This way, students can see what I expect them to do and create, but they will need to write all their own text.

> ✦✦ **Write an exemplar for the following prompt: Write a letter to your state representative that persuades them to pass a law requiring all students to wear purple clothes to school every day.**

## Try It Yourself

What types of assignments do you give to your students that might benefit from the addition of exemplars? Record your thoughts in the following space.

---

---

---

---

---

---

# Correcting One Another: Provide Structure for Peer Review and Grading

As powerful as self-assessment can be (see Looking in the Mirror, page 124), especially when combined with clear rubrics (see Setting Clear Expectations, page 126), one of the most impactful and underutilized practices in education is peer review (Sackstein, 2017). By sharing their work with their classmates and asking for feedback, students build critical-thinking skills while being exposed to diverse perspectives. They see their own work in a new light as well, often leading to improved performance. Most important, however, is the development of collaboration skills and reduced anxiety that come from working with others to fine-tune one's work. It's these skills that will prepare our students most for the careers that await them after school.

Peer review (also known as peer grading or peer feedback) is not as easy as simply pairing up your students to look at each other's work. For the time spent to be meaningful and productive, students need structures that will guide their work. They need protocols that can ensure that they know where they are going and can assess their progress. Generative AI chatbots are up to this task:

> ✦ ✦ **Create a procedure and handouts for my seventh-grade students to use when they review each other's lab reports.**

### Sample Output

Creating a peer review procedure and handouts for seventh-grade students reviewing each other's lab reports is a great way to encourage critical thinking and collaborative learning. Here's a suggested procedure along with handout content.

**Peer Review Procedure for Lab Reports**

**Objective:** To provide constructive feedback on lab reports, focusing on clarity, accuracy, and completeness.

**Materials Needed**

- Lab report copies for review
- Peer review handouts
- Pens or pencils

**Steps**

1. **Introducing Peer Review:**
   - Explain the purpose of peer review.
   - Emphasize the importance of constructive feedback.

2. **Pairing Up:**
   - Pair students randomly or in predetermined groups.
   - Each student should have a copy of their peer's lab report.

3. **Reviewing Guidelines:**
   - Distribute the peer review handouts.
   - Go over the handout, explaining each section.

4. **Reading and Reviewing:**
   - Students read their peer's lab report quietly.
   - They complete the handout, providing feedback based on the criteria.

**Discussion**

- Peers discuss the feedback, focusing on areas of improvement.
- Encourage respectful and helpful dialogue.

**Reflection**

Students reflect on the feedback received and plan for revisions.

**Teacher Review**

Collect the handouts for your own review to understand common issues.

**Peer Review Handout Content**

**Student Name:** _____       **Reviewer Name:** _____

**Lab Report Title:** _____

1. **Content Accuracy:**
   - Are the facts and concepts in the report accurate?
   - Rate the accuracy (1–5):

2. **Clarity of Writing:**
   - Is the report easy to understand?
   - Are there any confusing parts?
   - Suggestions for clarity:

3. **Completeness:**
   - Does the report cover all necessary parts (hypothesis, method, results, discussion)?
   - Note any missing elements:

4. **Data Presentation:**
   - Are the data and results presented clearly?
   - Are graphs and tables easy to interpret?
   - Suggestions for improvement:

5. **Logical Flow:**
   - Does the report follow a logical sequence?
   - Are the conclusions supported by the data?

6. **Grammar and Spelling:**
   - Note any grammar or spelling errors:

7. **Overall Impression:**
   - What did you like about the report?
   - What could be improved?

8. **Summary of Feedback:**
   - Provide a brief overall summary of your feedback.

**Tips for Teachers:**
- Encourage students to focus on positive aspects as well as areas for improvement.
- Monitor the discussions to ensure they remain respectful and constructive.
- Use the feedback to guide your teaching and address common issues in class.

This procedure and handout encourage a structured and positive peer review experience, helping students develop their analytical and communication skills.

This output provides not only a sample handout that is ready to be tweaked and printed out for students but also instructions for the teacher to use to structure the actual process of review. I don't think that I would use all the sections that the chatbot has included here, but it's a great starting point.

## Change It Up

There are several ways to make this prompt work for you and your classroom. First, consider how much structure you want your student pairs to have. Perhaps it makes sense to scale it down to a handful of areas to focus on:

> Create a procedure and handouts for my seventh-grade students to use when they review each other's lab reports. Focus on them reviewing each other's clarity, data, and analysis.

I find, in my own classroom, that feedback is most powerful (and most frequently acted on) when it is highly focused. I usually announce to the class which one or two elements of the assignment will be the emphasis of my grading and feedback. Giving students time to perform peer feedback on the same elements ensures that this practice has value for students and that you will receive high-quality submissions that have already been reviewed and edited before you see them.

If you are looking to save paper and streamline the peer-review process, consider creating a more visual tool for students to use:

> ✦✧ **Create a short checklist that my seventh-grade students can use to evaluate each other's lab reports. Use emoji and friendly language and make it able to fit on a half-page of paper.**

## Try It Yourself

Are your students skilled at peer review? If not, consider how you would like to begin to develop their ability to critically analyze each other's work. Record your thoughts in the following space.

---------------------------------------------------------------

---------------------------------------------------------------

---------------------------------------------------------------

---------------------------------------------------------------

---------------------------------------------------------------

# Showing You They Can Do It: Find Opportunities for Performance Assessment

An important facet of classroom assessment is the idea that the way that we choose to measure student learning should match the verb portion of the learning target (Stiggins & DuFour, 2009). For example, if a standard states that students must be able to *recall* a specific fact, we should test them by asking them to remember it. In the same way, if a learning standard requires that students be able to *measure* or *write* or *create*, the most effective and accurate classroom assessment will include students measuring, writing, or creating. This seems obvious at first glance but turns out to be very difficult in practice.

Performance assessment is time consuming and impractical on a large scale. It is often very difficult for the teacher to observe and provide feedback to more than a few students at a time as they attempt to demonstrate their skills. These assessments also require more manipulatives and other equipment than a more common multiple-choice or open-ended assessment would. These challenges leave educators in a bind: Do we choose the assessment format that is actually feasible given our time and classroom resources, or do we press on with authentic assessments that can be very tough to implement?

The best choice would seem to be a diverse assemblage of evaluations that combine those that teachers can administer and score easily with a small set of performance assessments that can provide truer student learning data. Our artificially intelligent teaching assistants can provide suggestions and draft assessments to make this process much less painful:

> My tenth-grade visual arts students are studying graphic design. Create a performance assessment that can be completed in thirty minutes or less that would measure their mastery of the principles of contrast, alignment, and proximity.

## Sample Output

For a performance assessment to measure your tenth-grade visual arts students' mastery of the principles of contrast, alignment, and proximity in graphic design within a thirty-minute timeframe, consider the following task.

**Assessment Title: "Mini Poster Design Challenge"**

**Objectives**
To evaluate students' understanding and application of contrast, alignment, and proximity in graphic design.

**Task**
Each student will design a mini poster (size A4) for a fictional event or product. The poster must prominently feature the principles of contrast, alignment, and proximity.

**Instructions**

1. **Theme Selection:** Students randomly pick a theme for their poster (for example, a music concert, book fair, new tech gadget, environmental campaign).

2. **Design Brief**
   - **Contrast:** Use color, typography, or size to create a focal point and hierarchy of information.
   - **Alignment:** Organize elements in a way that creates a clean and cohesive structure.
   - **Proximity:** Group related items together to establish clear relationships between them.

3. **Materials:** Students can use digital tools (like Adobe Illustrator or Photoshop) or traditional mediums (markers, pens, colored pencils) as per their preference and availability.

4. **Time Limit:** Thirty minutes of design time.

5. **Presentation:** After completion, each student will have a brief two-minute session to present their poster and explain how they incorporated the principles of contrast, alignment, and proximity.

**Assessment Criteria**

- **Creativity and Originality:** Innovation in theme interpretation and design approach.
- **Use of Contrast:** Effective use of contrast to create visual interest and hierarchy.
- **Alignment Mastery:** Clean, purposeful alignment that enhances readability and aesthetic appeal.
- **Proximity Principles:** Logical grouping of elements to convey clear relationships.
- **Overall Impact:** The overall visual appeal and communication effectiveness of the poster.

**Feedback**

- Provide individual feedback highlighting strengths and areas for improvement in each student's design.

This task not only assesses students' technical skills in applying these principles but also encourages creativity and quick thinking. It can be adapted to your classroom resources and the specific interests of your students.

Notice that this performance task includes elements of student choice to motivate students as well as a clear focus on the learning target. The assessment includes a presentation to give students an opportunity to explain how their work demonstrates the required skills. In some classes, it might make more sense to make this a recorded video or audio presentation or to have students reflect on paper to achieve a similar goal.

## Change It Up

If you're looking for ways to incorporate more performance assessment in your class, but you don't know where it fits, try asking the chatbot for ideas:

> ✦ I teach third-grade science, and I want to include more performance assessments. Give me ten ideas for performance assessments in my classroom.

Or, if you need tools for scoring student performances, the AI can help:

> ✦ Create a simple scoring sheet that I can use to grade my eleventh-grade civics students' performance assessment in which they held a mock trial.

## Try It Yourself

Use a generative AI tool to brainstorm some ways to use performance assessment in your class. Record your favorite responses in the following space.

--------------------------------------------------------------------------

--------------------------------------------------------------------------

--------------------------------------------------------------------------

--------------------------------------------------------------------------

--------------------------------------------------------------------------

--------------------------------------------------------------------------

--------------------------------------------------------------------------

--------------------------------------------------------------------------

## TIPS FOR TEAMS

Using AI models in the ways that I share throughout this book can help individual teachers streamline their work, but teams who work together to build content, measure student learning, and solve common challenges can benefit from another built-in feature of several of these tools: custom chatbots. As of July 2024, it is possible to create special bespoke chatbots using either ChatGPT (which calls them *GPTs*) or Claude (where they are called *Projects*) as part of their premium plans (Fitzpatrick, 2024). With both tools, teaching teams can upload documents like state learning standards, district or school curricula, existing lesson plans, and assessments, all of which are kept private and not used to train current and future models. Then, members of the team can ask the chatbot to answer questions or create materials with knowledge of those uploaded documents. By providing extensive context beforehand, outputs tend to be more accurate and relevant to the needs of the team. With their persistent memory and focused results, your team may find the benefits of these custom chatbots to outweigh the additional cost.

# Analyzing Student Work: Provide Automated Feedback to Students

By now, you have witnessed some of the amazing, creative tasks that generative AI models can carry out to help teachers. These tools achieve these goals by being able to read and interpret vast amounts of information, drawing connections and inferences among them (see Calling Tech Support in the introduction, page 2). We can tap into these analysis skills with a different type of prompt that includes attached examples of student work.

Remember that generative AI tools are based on large language models, which get their name from the enormous corpus of text and images on which they have trained (see Calling Tech Support in the introduction). While each model has a cutoff date after which it is no longer being actively trained, the companies that develop these models make it clear in their privacy notices that they maintain the right to use customer input to train future models (Google, 2024; OpenAI, 2023). This means that much of what we enter into a chatbot prompt may be stored and used later.

As educators, we are tasked with protecting not only our students but also their private data. Most schools have student data–privacy policies that preclude the sharing of identifiable information. Unless you are working with an AI tool that has been approved to handle this kind of data, it is very important that you and your team avoid including it in prompts that you submit to an AI. This may limit some of what you can do to automatically probe student work, but we must always put the safety of our students first. By taking care to scrub out any references to identifying information, we can safely recruit chatbots to help us provide feedback to students:

> Analyze this piece of student work [see figure 4.1, page 140, for the example I used, which is based on dozens of student responses to this assignment]. What does the student understand well? What do they need more support to master?

## Sample Output

The student work presented in the Chemical Reactions Lab Reflection shows an understanding of several key concepts but also displays areas where further support and clarification could be beneficial.

### Understanding Demonstrated

1. **Recognition of Chemical Reaction Signs:** The student can list the four signs of a chemical reaction: change of color, bubbling up, change of heat, and change of substance from solid to liquid.

2. **Effect of Ingredient Quantities:** They understand that the amount of substance used can affect the outcome of a reaction, as noted in the Color Change lab reflection.

**Chemical Reactions Lab Reflection**

Answer each question in the space to the right of it.

| | |
|---|---|
| What were the four signs of a chemical reaction that you witnessed during Labapalooza? | Change of color, bubbling up, change of heat, change of substance like solid to liquid |
| Which Labapalooza lab was the toughest lab for you? Why? | The first lab because I did not understand it |
| Which Labapalooza lab was your favorite? Why? | Lab 3 because it had the least work |
| During the Gas Formation lab, what did you learn about the effect of changing the amount of reactants? | I learned that the smallest change can affect everything like consistency of what it looks like |
| During the Temperature Change lab, what was your trick for getting the biggest change in temperature? | By using the most calcium chloride |
| During the Color Change lab, what would have happened if you added too much of the opposite to your unknown? How could you have fixed it? | If you put too little, it turns green, and if you add too much, it turns pink |
| During the Precipitate Formation lab, were you able to make any soap scum? How do you know? Why is it difficult to clean soap scum from surfaces in bathrooms? | It stays wet; therefore, it is harder to pick up |
| When you add Mentos candies to a bottle of Diet Coke, the carbon dioxide gas (bubbles) in the soda separates and shoots out of the soda bottle. Is this a chemical reaction? Why or why not? | Yes, this is a chemical reaction because ingredients in Coke and mentos react with each other, which is why it is a chemical reaction |
| A friend is getting confused about why some changes are chemical reactions. She doesn't get why melting ice is not a chemical reaction, while vinegar and baking soda making carbon dioxide gas is a chemical reaction. How would you explain it to her? | Because ice melting is the heat and there are no chemicals in heat. Baking soda and vinegar have chemicals in them that react, which is why it is a chemical reaction |

*Figure 4.1: Student work sample.*

3. **Identifying Chemical Reactions:** The student correctly identifies that the reaction between Diet Coke and Mentos is a chemical reaction due to the interaction of ingredients that produce gas bubbles.

## Areas for Further Support

### Understanding Chemical Principles

The student struggles with understanding why ice melting is not a chemical reaction. They need to learn that chemical reactions involve changes in the chemical composition of substances, whereas melting is a physical change that does not alter the chemical makeup of water.

They could benefit from a clearer explanation of what constitutes a chemical reaction, especially regarding the role of heat and the presence of chemicals. They seem to associate heat with the absence of chemical change, which is not accurate. Heat can be involved in both chemical and physical changes.

### Lab Comprehension

The student found the first lab tough because they did not understand it. They may need more foundational knowledge or a review of the concepts that lab was designed to teach.

They prefer labs with less work rather than considering the educational value or learning outcomes of the labs, which suggests they might benefit from understanding the purpose and goals of each lab activity more clearly.

### Analytical Skills

Their responses to how they would fix a problem during the Color Change Lab or how they would deal with precipitate formation are somewhat superficial and lack depth. Encouraging them to think through problems more critically and to consider multiple solutions could strengthen their problem-solving skills.

### Communication Skills

The explanation provided to the friend about why baking soda and vinegar react while ice melting does not may confuse someone without prior knowledge of chemistry. It's important to guide the student in providing clear, accurate explanations using appropriate scientific terminology.

## Suggestions for Support

- **Concept Reinforcement:** Review key concepts such as the differences between physical and chemical changes, and the role of heat in these processes.

- **Practical Demonstrations:** Conduct more hands-on activities where physical changes and chemical reactions can be observed and contrasted.

- **Reflection on Lab Activities:** Encourage the student to reflect more on the learning objectives of the lab activities rather than the workload involved.

- **Critical Thinking Exercises:** Provide exercises that require the student to apply what they've learned in hypothetical or real-world scenarios.

- **Guidance in Communication:** Teach the student how to communicate scientific concepts in a clear and accurate manner, potentially through peer teaching or presentation exercises.

The sample output from the prompt starts with what the student already knows and gives plenty of detail. This allows me to share those strengths with the student before moving on to the constructive feedback presented later in the output. The chatbot has also included suggestions for how a teacher could help support the student in closing the gaps in their mastery made evident by this work.

How can we make adjustments that will make this prompt work for other situations?

## Change It Up

We can use more specific language in our prompts to focus the feedback on a smaller set of target behaviors:

> Analyze this piece of student work. How well is the student able to demonstrate adding mixed numbers?

> Analyze this piece of student work. What are two quick tips for improvement?

In both cases, the goal is to minimize the quantity of feedback so that students don't feel overwhelmed by it. We know that students are much more likely to act on feedback that feels manageable, and bite-sized criticisms preceded by an expressed appreciation for the student's successes lead to more positive change (Ferriter & Cancellieri, 2017).

But what if you are looking to gain insight into the performance of an entire class? By attaching a spreadsheet of data (with student personal data removed), the AI can create both text summaries and graphs of the trends that it finds:

> Analyze this spreadsheet of student work from our grammar unit [see figure 4.2]. What trends do you see?

### Sample Output

Based on the spreadsheet you've provided, here are a few trends that can be observed from the grammar assessment data.

1. **General Improvement Over Time:** There seems to be a general trend of improvement for most students from assessment 1 to assessment 5. This suggests that the students are learning and retaining information about grammar over the course of the unit.

2. **Initial Performance Variance:** The starting levels (assessment 1) are quite varied, with scores ranging from 0.00 percent to 21.35 percent. This indicates a wide range of initial grammar skills among the students.

| Student_Grammar_Assessment_Data | | | | | |
|---|---|---|---|---|---|
| Student Name | Assessment 1 (Percent) | Assessment 2 (Percent) | Assessment 3 (Percent) | Assessment 4 (Percent) | Assessment 5 (Percent) |
| 1 | 18.82 | 15.56 | 30.00 | 40.05 | 53.30 |
| 2 | 12.00 | 10.10 | 27.90 | 48.93 | 52.04 |
| 3 | 14.83 | 18.26 | 21.85 | 40.63 | 46.15 |
| 4 | 21.20 | 20.78 | 32.31 | 42.01 | 52.70 |
| 5 | 19.34 | 26.15 | 25.46 | 49.42 | 46.63 |
| 6 | 51.10 | 26.01 | 30.26 | 33.26 | 50.16 |
| 7 | 14.75 | 18.00 | 33.66 | 33.65 | 46.82 |
| 8 | 9.24 | 18.49 | 30.04 | 44.85 | 53.30 |
| 9 | 0.48 | 14.76 | 35.70 | 34.13 | 52.88 |
| 10 | 12.05 | 12.80 | 23.83 | 40.72 | 48.96 |
| 11 | 10.72 | 11.47 | 32.01 | 37.93 | 51.98 |
| 12 | 17.27 | 29.75 | 26.58 | 36.26 | 44.53 |
| 13 | 13.81 | 17.45 | 25.65 | 49.61 | 42.54 |
| 14 | 10.61 | 17.81 | 27.11 | 47.40 | 52.20 |
| 15 | 12.22 | 13.74 | 28.44 | 49.34 | 50.83 |
| 16 | 11.67 | 23.89 | 30.28 | 44.53 | 53.18 |
| 17 | 17.47 | 11.93 | 24.17 | 35.69 | 61.92 |
| 18 | 9.70 | 18.94 | 34.50 | 54.72 | 54.72 |
| 19 | 11.57 | 15.52 | 32.33 | 30.66 | 45.44 |
| 20 | 5.73 | 21.90 | 22.32 | 44.01 | 55.59 |
| 21 | 0.00 | 17.45 | 37.44 | 44.74 | 43.42 |
| 22 | 13.27 | 14.10 | 35.40 | 30.22 | 47.05 |
| 23 | 14.32 | 19.86 | 35.89 | 43.07 | 49.66 |
| 24 | 6.29 | 22.14 | 29.10 | 44.61 | 58.57 |
| 25 | 21.35 | 20.33 | 24.65 | 41.88 | 46.28 |
| 26 | 2.73 | 21.51 | 35.27 | 34.50 | 45.87 |
| 27 | 10.23 | 16.83 | 27.98 | 41.49 | 49.51 |
| 28 | 9.06 | 18.19 | 36.11 | 46.63 | 46.48 |
| 29 | 17.66 | 16.64 | 31.04 | 36.53 | 55.63 |
| 30 | 17.35 | 18.20 | 34.88 | 39.25 | 44.60 |
| 31 | 10.77 | 15.93 | 31.78 | 37.82 | 44.26 |
| 32 | 11.89 | 11.37 | 33.53 | 49.25 | 47.81 |

*Figure 4.2:* Sample student assessment data.

3. **Significant Gains for Some Students:** Some students show significant gains between assessments. For example, Student 21 starts with a score of 0.00 percent and reaches 43.42 percent by assessment 5, indicating a remarkable improvement.

4. **Plateaus:** A few students exhibit plateauing, where their scores increase initially but then level off or fluctuate within a narrow range. For example, Student 8's scores fluctuate around the 30–50 percent range after the second assessment.

5. **High Achievers:** There are students who consistently score higher than others, such as Student 5, who starts at 19.34 percent and ends at 46.63 percent, never dropping below their initial score. This could indicate a strong foundation in grammar or effective study habits.

6. **Struggling Students:** Conversely, there are students who consistently score lower than the rest of the group, such as Student 20, who never scores above 55.59 percent. This might suggest a need for additional support or intervention.

7. **Inconsistencies:** Some students have inconsistent performances across the assessments. For instance, Student 13 has a score that rises and falls without a clear trend of improvement.

To gain more insights, it would be helpful to look at the content of each assessment to see if certain grammar topics are more challenging for students than others. Additionally, comparing these trends with classroom observations, homework performance, and other assessments could provide a more comprehensive picture of each student's understanding and skills in grammar.

## Try It Yourself

These prompts work best when you want a quick summary of the data provided, whether it be one student or an entire class. Can you envision a situation in your classroom where this would be helpful? Describe that situation in the following space.

-------------------------------------------------------------------

-------------------------------------------------------------------

-------------------------------------------------------------------

-------------------------------------------------------------------

-------------------------------------------------------------------

-------------------------------------------------------------------

-------------------------------------------------------------------

## Chapter Reflection

Every learning cycle reaches the point where you need to measure what students have learned before deciding what comes next. Just as the concepts that students are learning can vary, so must we vary the methods that we use to assess them. Working toward the goal of quick measurements that don't take away from the learning process and data that can be gathered easily and acted on immediately, we need to continuously evaluate the quality of our assessments.

We also must become more aware of the power that fair and supportive assessment has on the motivation of our students. When you make it clear to students that your goal with every test, project, and observation is to recognize their strengths and help them receive the support that they need to close any gaps, they begin to see assessment differently. They become less likely to cheat and more eager to get meaningful feedback and put it to use. In this way, your students become more ready for the challenges of 21st century careers.

To aid you in your quest to improve your assessment, in this chapter, we started by developing tools to help students prepare (Organizing and Studying). Then, we looked at ways to gather formative data efficiently (Getting Them Warmed Up, Capturing Quick Data, and Checking Out) to make on-demand instructional decisions. I shared techniques for developing metacognition and independence through self-assessment (Looking in the Mirror), peer assessment (Correcting One Another), and the use of rubrics and exemplars (Setting Clear Expectations and Showing What It Should Look Like). We reinforced the importance of authenticity by discussing performance assessment (Showing You They Can Do It). Finally, we explored the incredible ability of generative AI to crunch the numbers and help us find trends in student data (Analyzing Student Work).

In the final chapter, we will explore how we can use generative AI to help us navigate the learning cycle after we know which students need to extend their learning and which would benefit from some extra help.

# Chapter 4 Questions for Discussion

Using AI tools makes it much easier to expand your assessment toolkit. What is an assessment type or format that you do not use but may try out after using the prompts in this chapter? What advantage does this type of assessment offer?

How do you think the use of AI tools will impact the ways you use student data to plan instruction?

Looking at what is possible today, what new skills do you think that generative AI models will have in the coming years? How will this impact your work?

# CHAPTER 5

# Reteaching and Extension

✦ When people of all backgrounds consider the process of learning, they tend to use metaphors to describe it. One of the most common is that of running a race. We talk about *getting a good start* and *pacing ourselves* and *reaching for the finish line*. We worry about students being *behind* or *lapping* other students.

But educators know that true mastery follows a circular path. Students work their way through a learning cycle, reaching the expected level of proficiency at different points in time, often after repeated exposure to more challenging concepts (Bell, 2020). Ensuring that every student is successful means providing on-demand reteaching for those who need some extra time and practice while also giving expert students a chance to stretch themselves into a more advanced understanding of the content.

Crafting meaningful and effective learning experiences for students in both groups can be enormously time-consuming, which is why many classroom teachers simply forgo reteaching and extension altogether. Creating additional resources for the students who have not met expected mastery is not *extra* work, though; it *is* the work. If those students do not learn the content, we have not completely accomplished what we set out to do. We also have an ethical obligation to our students who reach mastery and need to feed their desire to learn. As we've seen already, this is a great opportunity to let an AI chatbot do much of the hard work for us. In this chapter, we explore prompts that can make helpful resources for both remediation and enrichment.

## Figuring Out How to Help: Brainstorm Strategies for Struggling Students

Sometimes we are tasked with helping students in subjects with which we are not familiar. Or we feel that we have exhausted all the techniques that we have to teach a specific topic. We can lean again on the generative AI chatbot to help produce a list of ideas:

> ✦✦ **How can I help a student who is struggling to understand arithmetic sequences?**

## Sample Output

Helping a student who is struggling to understand arithmetic sequences requires patience, clear explanations, and various teaching strategies. Here are some tips to assist the student.

1. **Identify the Specific Difficulties:** Talk to the student and find out exactly what they are struggling with. It could be understanding the concept itself, solving problems, or applying the formula. Knowing their specific challenges will help you tailor your assistance.

2. **Start With the Basics:** Ensure the student has a solid foundation in basic arithmetic, including addition and subtraction. Review these concepts if necessary, as they are essential for understanding arithmetic sequences.

3. **Define Arithmetic Sequences:** Begin by explaining what an arithmetic sequence is, emphasizing that it's a sequence of numbers with a constant difference between consecutive terms.

4. **Visual Aids:** Use visual aids like number lines or graphs to illustrate arithmetic sequences. Visual representations can help students grasp the concept better.

5. **Real-World Examples:** Show practical examples of arithmetic sequences in everyday life, such as counting money, telling time, or measuring distances. This can make the concept more relatable and understandable.

Remember that every student learns differently, so be flexible in your approach and try different strategies to find what works best for the individual. Building a strong understanding of arithmetic sequences can pave the way for success in more advanced mathematical concepts.

The goal of brainstorming is to nonjudgmentally produce a big list of ideas and then whittle them down by filtering out the ones that are not useful for our given circumstances. I've included the first five suggestions here to convey what to expect, but the original output included fourteen ideas. I find these suggestions to be a great starting point for planning a round of reteaching or remediation for students who didn't master this topic the first time.

## Change It Up

Right away, it makes sense to modify this prompt to fit the characteristics of my classroom, like the size of the group or the tools available:

> ✦✦ **How can I help a student who is struggling to understand arithmetic sequences in a small-group setting?**

> ✦ How can I help a student who is struggling to understand arithmetic sequences using my interactive whiteboard?

Or, we can select a type of strategy and have the AI provide some advice about using it to reteach a specific topic:

> ✦ How can I use stations to help a student who is struggling to understand arithmetic sequences?

## Try It Yourself

Pick a topic that you have taught recently and use a prompt like the ones in this section to generate some ideas for reteaching. Capture the best ones in the following space.

-------------------------------------------------------------

-------------------------------------------------------------

-------------------------------------------------------------

-------------------------------------------------------------

-------------------------------------------------------------

-------------------------------------------------------------

-------------------------------------------------------------

-------------------------------------------------------------

-------------------------------------------------------------

-------------------------------------------------------------

-------------------------------------------------------------

-------------------------------------------------------------

-------------------------------------------------------------

## TIPS FOR TEAMS

To ensure that we never treat reteaching or enrichment as optional parts of the learning cycle, we need to leverage the power of working together—with AI tools and with each other. If your team does not already have a shared space to warehouse materials that you have created together or share with one another, you should do that right away. Consider online storage with collaborative features like Google Drive (https://drive.google.com) or Microsoft OneDrive (https://onedrive.microsoft.com). Organize it by instructional standard, perhaps using the same numbering system that your state or district employs. For each learning target, include a folder for remediation resources and one for extension activities. As you create, fine-tune, and use materials (including those inspired by the prompts in this book), drop them into that shared digital filing cabinet. That way, when you need a way to remediate or enrich students in the future, a vetted tool will be waiting for you.

The same folder system can be used to keep track of the AI chatbot prompts that your team members have used, along with how you have learned to modify them successfully. Consider keeping a document inside the folder for each unit that lists the prompts that your team found useful for that unit. As you build out these resources, make use of the commenting feature of tools like Microsoft Word or Google Docs to annotate the prompts with notes about how you have used them and what you liked—and didn't like—about their outputs.

## Breaking It Down: Craft Simple Explainers for Remediation

In my classroom, when a student is unsuccessful in understanding a concept or mastering a skill during the initial teaching stage, it is usually caused by a lack of sufficient language skills (reading below grade level or multilingual learner) needed to comprehend the lesson. As a result, my best tool is often a simplified explanation of the concept. This explanation can be presented verbally or aurally for students to hear or in written form at a reading level that is appropriate for their skills. As we've seen before (see Leaning Into Literacy in chapter 2, page 49), generative AI models excel at producing customized text passages. We can use a version of that type of prompt here as well:

> Give me a short explanation of color theory for a student at the second-grade level.

### Sample Output

Sure! Color theory is a fun way to understand colors and how they work together. Colors are all around us, like in the clothes we wear, the pictures we draw, and the world we see.

There are three primary colors: red, blue, and yellow. These colors are special because you can't mix other colors together to create them. But guess what? When you mix two primary colors, you get a new color! For example, when you mix red and blue, you get purple. When you mix blue and yellow, you get green. And when you mix red and yellow, you get orange.

Besides the primary colors, there are also secondary colors: purple, green, and orange. Now, if you mix a primary color with a secondary color, you get something called a tertiary color. Tertiary colors are made by mixing a primary color with a secondary color next to it. For example, if you mix red with orange, you get a reddish-orange color.

Colors can also have different feelings or moods. For instance, red can make you feel excited or energetic, while blue might make you feel calm and relaxed. Artists and designers use colors in special ways to create beautiful and meaningful pictures or designs.

Remember, colors are amazing, and playing with them is a wonderful way to explore and express your creativity! Have fun learning about the colorful world around you!

When reteaching a topic to students who didn't master it initially, it's important to use different techniques and different resources to maximize their ability to find the way that sticks for them (Bellert, 2015). Simple text passages like this one can be annotated or discussed in pairs or plugged into text-to-audio tools to create spoken explanations, too.

## Change It Up

If you have an idea of which part of a topic is difficult for the students to understand, you can add those details to the prompt:

> **Give me a short explanation of color theory for a student at the second-grade level, with a focus on combining colors.**

Or, adjust the prompt to get an explanation of just the right length for the students you will be using it with:

> **Give me a two-paragraph explanation of color theory for a student at the second-grade level.**

Or, even add some graphical elements to enhance the readability of the text and engagement of your students:

> ✦ Give me a short explanation of color theory for a student at the second-grade level. Include emoji to make the passage more interesting.

## Try It Yourself

When providing remediation time with students, it's frequently true that you will have different groups of students with different gaps in their understanding. This type of prompt can quickly create customized resources for each. What's a topic that you teach that leads to different misconceptions or incomplete understandings among your students?

----------------------------------------

----------------------------------------

----------------------------------------

----------------------------------------

----------------------------------------

----------------------------------------

# Reteaching Them: Design Reteaching Resources

Sometimes, during the process of gathering assessment data and observing student learning, it becomes clear that student misunderstanding is caused by gaps in their earlier learning. As the educator familiar with this year's learning targets and content, you might not have easy access to lessons and strategies for closing gaps in prior knowledge. An AI chatbot can help you explore some possibilities:

> ✦ Give me an activity to reteach two-digit multiplication to a student who is not very adept at multiplication.

### Sample Output

Sure! Here's an activity designed to reteach two-digit multiplication to a student who may be struggling with multiplication:

**Activity: Multiplication Bingo**

**Objective:** The objective of this activity is to reinforce two-digit multiplication skills through a fun and engaging bingo game.

**Materials Needed**
- Bingo cards (premade or create your own grid)
- Small pieces of paper or tokens
- Multiplication table (cheat sheet) for reference
- Pencils or markers

**Instructions**

1. **Prepare Bingo Cards:**
   - Create bingo cards with a 4 × 4 grid. In each square, write a two-digit multiplication problem (for example, 23 × 12) or the result of a two-digit multiplication problem (for example, 276).
   - Ensure that each bingo card has a different arrangement of multiplication problems or results.

2. **Review the Multiplication Table:**
   - Before starting the game, go over the multiplication table with the student. Focus on the multiplication facts they struggle with the most. You can create a small multiplication table cheat sheet for them to use during the game.

3. **Distribute the Bingo Cards:**
   - Give each student a bingo card and a pencil or marker.

4. **Draw Multiplication Problems:**
   - As the facilitator, you will draw one multiplication problem at a time from a container (a bowl or bag). For example, you might draw a piece of paper that says, "23 × 12."

5. **Solve the Multiplication Problem:**
   - Ask the student to solve the multiplication problem quietly on their card. If they need help, encourage them to use the multiplication table cheat sheet.

This lesson includes the baked-in engagement of a game with explicit practice that can be customized for each student or group of students. But you might want to adjust it to match your timeframe or student group size.

## Change It Up

By adding some more specifics to the prompt, you can get exactly what you need:

> ✦✦ Give me an activity to reteach two-digit multiplication in ten minutes to a student who is not very adept at multiplication.

> ✦✦ Give me an activity to reteach two-digit multiplication to a group of two students who are not very adept at multiplication.

Both modified prompts will create completely different activities that are focused on the limitations that you add. By using them together, you can even produce multiple activities that can be used as rotating stations for students who need additional support.

## Try It Yourself

Think back to a time when you had multiple students who needed extra help with closing gaps in prior knowledge from previous units or years of instruction. What resources would have made it easier for you to help those students? Brainstorm some ideas in the following space.

---------------------------------------------------------------

---------------------------------------------------------------

---------------------------------------------------------------

---------------------------------------------------------------

---------------------------------------------------------------

---------------------------------------------------------------

---------------------------------------------------------------

---------------------------------------------------------------

---------------------------------------------------------------

---------------------------------------------------------------

# Using a Video Better: Match Reteaching Videos With Video Guides

Another effective way to reteach a concept is what my colleague Bill Ferriter calls "reteaching without a teacher" (W. Ferriter, personal communication, May 5, 2010) using tools like Edpuzzle to add questions to videos. Video-hosting sites like YouTube include hundreds of high-quality educational videos. By using video transcripts when they are available and accurate (auto-generated ones often have problems) combined with AI, you can create thoughtful questions easily. Start by highlighting and copying the transcript from the video's YouTube page (click on ". . . more" and then "Show transcript" at the end of the video description). The sample here is from "What Color Are Stars?"

on the SciShow Kids (2021) YouTube channel. Then, add it to a prompt to make an easy viewing guide:

> ✦✦ **Create a set of five questions about this video.**
> **[Insert transcript text]**

### Sample Output

1. What is the person in the video observing, and how are they able to see stars on the fort's screen?

2. Why did the person in the video think that all stars would be yellow, and what surprised them when they looked more closely at the stars?

3. How do the colors of stars indicate their temperature, and what is the general relationship between a star's color and its temperature?

4. What color is the sun, and how does its temperature compare to that of other stars in the video?

5. Why would it be really hot near a blue star, and how does the temperature of a blue star compare to that of a red star?

Notice that the chatbot doesn't need to "see" the video if it can access the transcript. The questions that it generates measure student recall of facts from the video. This is sometimes a great way to ensure that students pay attention to it, but it doesn't foster deeper learning or ensure that students truly comprehend the lessons in the video. For that, we need to make some changes.

## Change It Up

To make the video guides more effective and more comprehensive, try asking the chatbot for different types of questions:

> ✦✦ **Create a set of five questions about this video: [Insert transcript].**
> **Ensure that some of the questions are open ended and require**
> **clear understanding of the video concepts.**

> ✦✦ **Create a task about this video that will require students to**
> **summarize the critical information in it: [Insert transcript]**

And don't forget that you can ask the chatbot to provide suggested responses or an answer key to any questions that it writes.

## Try It Yourself

Find a video that you would use for remediation and practice getting the transcript and using it in an AI prompt. What were the sticking points? How might you use this in your classroom? Record your answers in the following space.

------------------------------------------------------------

------------------------------------------------------------

------------------------------------------------------------

------------------------------------------------------------

------------------------------------------------------------

------------------------------------------------------------

------------------------------------------------------------

------------------------------------------------------------

# Listening to Learn: Find and Maximize Educational Podcasts

The podcast format is not new, but the resurgence that began in 2014 (St. Aubin, 2023) has led to the creation of many high-quality audio lessons that teachers can integrate into classroom learning, especially for remediation. Studies reveal that audio instruction activates parts of our memory system that can lead to better recall (Bent, McShea, & Brennan, 2015). Searching the internet for relevant podcasts and making instructional materials to accompany them is no small task, but it can yield enormous benefits for students. Let's see how a generative AI tool can make it easier:

> ✦ Find a podcast episode that could be used to help ninth-grade students understand how climate change is connected to carbon. Create three questions for students to reflect on the episode after listening.

### Sample Output

For ninth-grade students learning about how climate change is connected to carbon, the podcast episode "E5: Wildfires—And How We're Changing Them" from *TILclimate* (*Today I Learned: Climate*) by MIT would be an excellent resource. This award-winning podcast breaks down the science, technologies, and policies behind climate change, making it accessible and informative for students. The episode in question explores the topic of wildfires and human impact on them, which ties into the broader theme of climate change and carbon emissions (https://climate.mit.edu /tilclimate-podcast).

After listening to the episode, students could reflect on the following questions.

**How do wildfires relate to climate change and carbon emissions?**

This question encourages students to make connections between the specific topic of wildfires discussed in the episode and the broader issue of climate change, particularly focusing on how carbon emissions play a role.

**What are some of the key takeaways from the episode regarding human impact on climate change?**

This question prompts students to think critically about human activities and their contribution to climate change, as highlighted in the podcast episode.

**How can the information in this episode guide our daily decisions or actions regarding environmental conservation and carbon footprint reduction?**

This reflective question aims to connect the theoretical knowledge from the podcast to practical, everyday actions. It encourages students to think about how they can apply what they have learned to make a positive impact on the environment.

These questions are designed to stimulate critical thinking and help students integrate the information they have learned from the podcast into a broader understanding of climate change and its connection to carbon emissions.

The chatbot performed an internet search and then presented the top result with a summary and explanation. Obviously, you would need to preview the podcast to ensure that it meets learning targets and is appropriate for your students. But by combining the steps of searching, evaluating podcasts, and creating teaching materials, AI can save you a lot of time. With some small tweaks, you can make the output from the prompt even more useful.

## Change It Up

When assessing whether the output of a prompt is going to meet the needs of my students, I prefer to have multiple options to choose from. An important change to consider is asking the chatbot for three or more choices and, after previewing them, either trimming the list down to the best option or offering students the choice:

> ✦ **Find three podcast episodes that could be used to help sixth-grade students understand how technology is changing the way people exercise.**

You can also ask the chatbot to produce one or more ideas for creative assignments related to a podcast episode:

> ✦✦ Find a podcast episode that could be used to help ninth-grade
> students understand how climate change is connected to carbon.
> Create a project for a group of two to four students that would
> allow them to demonstrate a deeper understanding of the content.

## Try It Yourself

Even if you don't listen to podcasts yourself, they represent a powerful medium for student learning. Find a podcast that you would use with your students and reflect on its potential in the following space.

---

---

---

---

---

---

---

## Letting Them Create: Use Maker Activities to Enhance Student Engagement

Sometimes spending more time in the learning cycle to improve mastery can feel like a slog to students. When this happens, motivation wanes, and reteaching becomes less effective. One of the best ways to keep these students engaged is to let them be creators (Halverson & Sheridan, 2014). Using a good prompt helps you design activities in which students make products to show their freshly improved level of mastery:

> ✦✦ What's a creative product that struggling third-grade students can
> create to show that they understand the fitness knowledge and
> skills to maintain a health-enhancing lifestyle?

## Sample Output

A creative product that struggling third-grade students can create to show their understanding of fitness knowledge and skills to maintain a health-enhancing lifestyle is a Fitness and Health Journal. Here's how it can be structured.

### Fitness and Health Journal

1. **Cover Page**
   Students can design a colorful cover page with their name and a title such as "My Fitness and Health Journal."

2. **Daily Activity Log**
   A simple log where students record their daily physical activities. They can draw or write about the activities they did each day (e.g., playing tag, riding a bike, dancing).

3. **Healthy Eating Diary**
   A section for students to draw or list the healthy foods they ate during the week. They can include pictures or cutouts from magazines to make it more engaging.

4. **Fitness Goals**
   A page where students set simple fitness goals for themselves, such as "I will jump rope for 10 minutes every day" or "I will try a new vegetable each week."

5. **Exercise Illustrations**
   Students can draw themselves doing different exercises or activities they enjoy, like jumping jacks, running, or swimming. They can also label the muscles used in each activity if they are ready for a bit more challenge.

6. **Healthy Habits Checklist**
   A checklist of healthy habits to maintain a healthy lifestyle, such as drinking water, getting enough sleep, and brushing their teeth. Students can check off each habit as they complete it.

7. **Reflection Pages**
   Pages for students to reflect on how they felt after their activities. They can use smiley faces or simple sentences to express their feelings and thoughts.

8. **Family Fitness Fun**
   A section where students can plan a family fitness activity, like a walk in the park or a family sports day. They can describe or draw what they plan to do and how it will help everyone stay healthy.

This journal not only allows students to demonstrate their understanding of fitness and health concepts but also encourages them to practice these skills in a fun and engaging way.

I really like this idea of combining something that has proven utility (a fitness log) with an engaging format that will draw students in. I think that my students would be motivated to complete this, and that students who need some extra exposure to the content would receive it without the sense of dread that sometimes accompanies remediation.

## Change It Up

How can we adjust this prompt to get ideas that would work in other classroom situations? There are tons of ways to mix up these "reteach and create" prompts, ranging from defining the type of product to creating choice boards with multiple options:

> ✦ **What's a Google Slides product that struggling third-grade students can create to show that they understand the fitness knowledge and skills to maintain a health-enhancing lifestyle?**

> ✦ **What's a set of nine short creative products that struggling third-grade students can create to show that they understand the fitness knowledge and skills to maintain a health-enhancing lifestyle?**

Think about the limitations of your classroom (for example, technology availability or access to craft supplies) when planning activities like this and feed those constraints to the AI model as you adapt the prompt.

## Try It Yourself

Making a physical product of their relearning experience is a powerful way for students to retain the new knowledge and better apply it on future assessments. What's a topic that you teach that would lend itself to creative remediation activities? Capture it in the following space.

-------------------------------------------------------------------

-------------------------------------------------------------------

-------------------------------------------------------------------

-------------------------------------------------------------------

-------------------------------------------------------------------

-------------------------------------------------------------------

-------------------------------------------------------------------

-------------------------------------------------------------------

# Centering the Mind: Minimize Stress Through Mindfulness

All students (or humans, for that matter) benefit from the reduction of stress and the ability to focus one's mind inward. Sadly, mindfulness practices (which include meditation and self-awareness) are not taught in many classrooms. While all students need more mindfulness, studies have shown that students in more advanced classes and those who put pressure on themselves to excel suffer more from stress and depression than the average (Bostic et al., 2015). We owe it to them to show the power of mindfulness in our classes. Generative AI tools can help us create mindful activities that do not require very much time to plan or to implement:

> ✦ Create three simple mindfulness exercises for a third-grade classroom.

## Sample Output

Certainly! Mindfulness exercises for third graders should be simple, engaging, and suitable for their age. Here are three exercises that can be easily implemented in a third-grade classroom:

1. **Mindful Breathing With a Stuffed Animal**

   - **Objective:** To help students focus on their breathing in a fun and relatable way.

   - **How to Do It:**
     - Each student gets a small stuffed animal (or they can imagine one).
     - They lie down and place the stuffed animal on their belly.
     - They watch the stuffed animal rise and fall as they breathe in and out.
     - Guide them to notice how the animal moves up with each inhale and down with each exhale.
     - Do this for two to three minutes, encouraging them to focus solely on their breathing and the movement of the stuffed animal.

2. **Mindful Listening**

   - **Objective:** To enhance listening skills and awareness of sounds in the environment.

   - **How to Do It:**
     - Have the students sit quietly and close their eyes.
     - Play a series of different sounds (like a bell, rustling leaves, or gentle music).
     - Ask them to raise their hand when they hear a sound and then lower it when the sound stops.
     - After listening to a few different sounds, ask them to describe what they heard and how it made them feel.
     - This exercise can last about five minutes.

3. **The Gratitude Moment**

   - **Objective:** To foster a sense of gratitude and positive thinking.

- **How to Do It:**
  - Have the students sit in a comfortable position.
  - Ask them to think of one thing they are grateful for. It could be a person, a place, an object, or an experience.
  - Give them a moment to reflect on why they are grateful for this thing.
  - If they are comfortable, allow them to share their gratitude with the class.
  - This exercise helps students focus on positive aspects of their lives and can last for about five minutes.

These exercises are designed to be simple yet effective, helping young students to develop mindfulness skills in a way that's enjoyable and age appropriate.

These three activities could each be useful in different situations. I can imagine using variations of each of them at different times in my classroom.

## Change It Up

You may decide that something on a smaller scale works better for you and your students. Consider these tweaks:

> ✦✦ **Create three simple mindfulness exercises for a ninth-grade classroom that students could do independently.**

These activities could be given to students just before an enrichment activity to aid with stress reduction. To integrate these mindfulness activities into your lessons, and make them feel less like a digression, you could infuse them with elements of your curriculum:

> ✦✦ **Create a simple mindfulness exercise for students who are studying the Revolutionary War.**

### Sample Output

A mindfulness exercise tailored for students studying the Revolutionary War can incorporate elements of history to make it more engaging and relevant. Here's a simple exercise.

**Mindfulness Exercise: Revolutionary War Reflection**

**Duration:** 10–15 minutes

**Materials Needed:** Quiet space, comfortable seating, and optional calming background music.

**Instructions**

1. **Settle In:** Have students find a comfortable seated position. Encourage them to close their eyes and take three deep, slow breaths.

2. **Guided Imagery—Time Travel:** Guide the students to imagine themselves traveling back in time to the Revolutionary War era. Encourage them to envision the landscapes, clothing, and atmosphere of that period.

3. **Observing the Senses:**
   - **Sight**—Ask them to imagine observing a scene from the Revolutionary War. It could be a battlefield, a colonial town, or a meeting of the founding fathers.
   - **Sound**—Let them imagine the sounds they might hear—perhaps the distant rumble of cannons, the hustle and bustle of a colonial market, or the passionate speeches of leaders.
   - **Smell**—Encourage them to think about the smells of the era—the musky scent of wood, the smoke from a fireplace, or the fresh country air.

4. **Connecting With Emotions:** Ask students to reflect on what emotions they might feel if they were living in that time. What struggles and hopes might they have? This encourages empathy and understanding of the historical context.

5. **Bringing Lessons to the Present:** Guide students to think about what lessons from the Revolutionary War era can be applied today. Ask them to consider values like freedom, resilience, and unity.

6. **Returning to the Present:** Slowly guide students back to the present. Ask them to take a few deep breaths and gradually open their eyes.

7. **Group Reflection:** Open a discussion where students can share their experience, insights, or any emotions that the exercise brought up.

This exercise helps students to connect more deeply with the subject they are studying, while also providing a moment of calm and reflection in their day.

What a neat way to keep students in the mindset of the content they're learning while also teaching them to use breathing exercises and visualization to manage stress.

## Try It Yourself

Whether you are an active practitioner of mindfulness or a novice, the best way to experiment with these types of activities is to try them yourself before using them with students. So, pick a prompt from this section and record your reflections about its usefulness in the following space.

-------------------------------------------------------------------------------

-------------------------------------------------------------------------------

-------------------------------------------------------------------------------

-------------------------------------------------------------------------------

-------------------------------------------------------------------------------

## Writing to Learn: Generate Writing Prompts to Push Student Thinking

When students reach a solid level of mastery early in a learning cycle, it's important to keep their interest and motivation rolling by giving them activities and resources that extend from where they are (Reis & Renzulli, 2010). Try giving these students a chance to apply what they have learned in new ways. Creative composition is a proven method for sparking more complex assimilation of classroom learning targets (Dai, 2012). There's also a handy way to make sure that your writing prompts (and other AI output) are closely aligned to your learning targets: copy and paste text from the state or district standards into your prompt. For example, in looking for writing prompts for middle school students in a North Carolina social studies class, I identified standard 6.B.1.1—"Explain how religion, tradition, and cultural practice influence the development of civilizations and societies in Africa, Asia, Europe and the Americas" (North Carolina Department of Public Instruction, n.d.)—and then incorporated it into the request to the AI chatbot:

> Create three writing prompts for sixth-grade students to show that they can explain how religion, tradition, and cultural practice influence the development of civilizations and societies in Africa, Asia, Europe, and the Americas.

### Sample Output

1. **Religion's Role in Shaping Civilizations:** Choose a civilization from Africa, Asia, Europe, or the Americas and describe how religion influenced its development. Discuss specific religious beliefs, practices, and institutions, and explain how these elements affected the society's laws, education, art, and government. Provide examples to support your explanation.

2. **Tradition and Cultural Practices Across Continents:** Compare and contrast the role of tradition and cultural practices in two different civilizations, one from Africa or Asia and one from Europe or the Americas. Explain how these traditions and practices helped shape the social structure, daily life, and identity of each civilization. Highlight both similarities and differences in their influences.

3. **Cultural Exchange and Its Impact on Societies:** Explore how the exchange of cultural practices, traditions, or religious beliefs between civilizations from different continents (Africa, Asia, Europe, or the Americas) influenced their development. Discuss specific examples of cultural exchange, such as trade, conquest, or exploration, and explain how these interactions led to changes in social, economic, or political structures.

By including some of the language from the state curriculum standards in the prompt, I was able to get the chatbot to create writing prompts closely aligned to what students have learned in class. Remember that you can (and should) always review the output for its appropriateness before assigning it to students. It's also important to make sure that the rigor and difficulty of the writing prompt push students without frustrating them.

## Change It Up

There are many types of writing, and you can make changes to the prompt to ask students to create different kinds of work. If you're concerned that students will not understand how to write in a particular style, ask the chatbot to provide examples to guide them:

> Create three writing prompts for middle school students to show that they understand the differences and similarities of cultures around the world are attributable to their diverse origins and histories, and interactions with other cultures throughout time, using a rhyming poem format. Explain the format with examples.

This type of prompt gives you output that marries the earlier creative writing activities with the power of exemplars (as I discussed in Showing What It Should Look Like in chapter 4, page 129). Advanced students benefit greatly from instructions that provide an example of the end product, but leave open the opportunity to make independent decisions (Smyth & Carless, 2021).

## Try It Yourself

Experiment with the prompt ideas in this section to create some interesting and thought-provoking creative writing prompts. Record your best examples in the following sections.

## Seeing Where We're Going: Identify Which Learning Targets Come Next in a Vertical Sequence

Many educators who know their own curriculum well do not have a lot of familiarity with the standards and concepts for levels beyond where they teach. However, connecting future courses to the work that students are mastering now can be a very strong motivator to encourage extended learning. It can provide a sense of purpose for students who want to be successful in later courses and need to connect to what they are learning now:

> ✦ How do Newton's Laws of Motion connect with high school science?

### Sample Output

Newton's Laws of Motion are fundamental principles in classical mechanics that describe the relationship between the motion of an object and the forces acting upon it. These laws form a cornerstone of high school science education as they help students understand the basic principles behind various physical phenomena they encounter in their daily lives. Here's how Newton's Laws connect with high school science:

1. **First Law of Motion (Law of Inertia)**

   - **Description:** An object at rest stays at rest, and an object in motion continues in motion with the same speed and in the same direction unless acted upon by an external force.

   - **High School Science Connection:** This law explains the concept of inertia, the tendency of objects to resist changes in their state of motion. Students can relate this to real-life scenarios, such as why they need to wear seat belts in a car to prevent being thrown forward when the car suddenly stops.

2. **Second Law of Motion (Law of Acceleration)**

   - **Description:** The acceleration of an object is directly proportional to the net force acting on it and inversely proportional to its mass. The direction of the acceleration is the same as the direction of the net force.

   - **High School Science Connection:** This law provides a mathematical framework to understand how force, mass, and acceleration are related. Students learn to calculate acceleration and understand why larger forces are needed to accelerate more massive objects at the same rate as less massive ones.

3. **Third Law of Motion (Action-Reaction Law)**

   - **Description:** For every action, there is an equal and opposite reaction. Whenever one object exerts a force on a second object, the second object exerts an equal and opposite force back on the first object.

- **High School Science Connection:** This law helps explain interactions between objects and is often demonstrated through examples like rockets launching, where the expelled gases in one direction (action) propel the rocket in the opposite direction (reaction). Students also learn about the normal force and tension force as reactions to weight and other applied forces.

The Laws of Motion provide a framework to understand and predict the behavior of objects in response to forces. Students use these laws to solve problems involving motion, forces, and equilibrium. Additionally, these laws form the basis for more advanced topics in physics and engineering, making them an essential foundation for further scientific studies in high school and beyond.

Furthermore, the Laws of Motion are often taught along with practical experiments and demonstrations, such as inclined planes, pulleys, and collisions, to provide students with hands-on experience and a deeper understanding of these principles. Overall, Newton's Laws of Motion play a crucial role in shaping students' comprehension of classical mechanics and developing their scientific reasoning skills.

This output shares information that both students and teachers can use. I have used information like this to create cover pages for packets of enrichment work, connecting the new work with students' desire to excel in future subjects. I look for text that my students can read with some challenge as well as reasoning that would motivate my students.

## Change It Up

If you're looking for more connections narrowed down more by topic, consider adding more detail to the prompt:

> How does inertia come up again in high school physics?

Or, if you know that your students would be more motivated by a sense of the interconnectedness between subjects in school, ask the chatbot to provide more horizontal (cross-curricular) alignment:

> How do Newton's Laws of Motion connect with other middle school subjects?

## Try It Yourself

Pick a topic that you teach and use one of the prompts in this section to create vertical connections with future coursework. How would your more advanced students react to this type of activity? Reflect in the following space.

---

---

---

---

---

---

---

# Beating the Bot: Build Deeper Understanding by Finding Mistakes

One of the more advanced skills that students develop when learning a new topic is the ability to recognize and correct errors in one another's work (Perry, Lundie, & Golder, 2019). John Perry, David Lundie, and Gill Golder (2019) explain that many students are naturally motivated when tasked with finding mistakes, and it can activate parts of the brain that lead to deeper comprehension. While we have seen how effective AI tools are at creating educational text, recall from the introduction (page 1) that these large language models do sometimes make factual errors. Combining these two ideas, one great way to build stronger understanding of a topic that some students have mastered is to have them critique AI-produced text, looking for and correcting mistakes. To ensure a useful educational experience, ask the AI to include mistakes. Start with a simple prompt to generate some relevant text, the more specific the better:

> ✦ **Describe the differences between tap dance and Bollywood dance styles. Include some errors in your explanation.**

### Sample Output

Tap dance and Bollywood dance styles are both unique forms of dance, but they differ in several ways.

1. **Origin:** Tap dance originated in India during ancient times and later spread to the United States during the 19th century. On the other hand, Bollywood dance style originated in the United States and gained popularity in India during the 20th century.

2. **Footwork:** In tap dance, dancers wear special shoes with metal plates on the soles that create rhythmic sounds when they strike the floor. The tapping sound is an essential element of tap dance. In Bollywood dance, footwork is more focused on intricate and graceful movements, emphasizing storytelling through dance gestures.

3. **Music:** Tap dance is traditionally performed to jazz or blues music, and the rhythm of the dance is closely connected to the music's beats. Bollywood dance, on the other hand, is performed to the tunes of popular Bollywood songs, which are usually a mix of Indian classical, folk, and contemporary music.

4. **Movements:** Tap dance incorporates a lot of swift and intricate foot movements, with dancers often seen tapping in syncopated rhythms. Bollywood dance, on the contrary, incorporates a wide range of movements that include not only footwork but also expressive hand gestures, facial expressions, and energetic jumps.

5. **Costumes:** Tap dance costumes are usually more conservative, with dancers wearing formal attire that allows for ease of movement and tapping. Bollywood dance costumes, on the other hand, are vibrant and extravagant, often featuring colorful, sequined outfits that reflect the exuberance of Indian culture.

6. **Choreography:** Tap dance routines are characterized by complex and intricate footwork sequences, with a strong emphasis on syncopation and rhythm. Bollywood dance choreography often involves group formations, storytelling elements, and a blend of traditional Indian dance styles like Kathak and Bhangra.

7. **Cultural Influence:** While tap dance has its roots in American and Indian cultures, Bollywood dance is a fusion of various Indian dance forms and Western influences. Bollywood dance often incorporates elements of hip-hop, jazz, and contemporary dance styles.

Overall, both tap dance and Bollywood dance are captivating and entertaining dance forms that showcase the rich cultural heritage of their respective origins. Their differences in music, footwork, movements, costumes, and choreography contribute to their distinct styles and appeal to different audiences worldwide.

Once you have a section of text with included errors, create the opportunity for students to work independently or in small groups to read the text closely and try to find the errors. When I use the strategy with my own students, I like to add the challenge of annotating printed copies of the text with corrections to the errors. I find that my students read the text and analyze it so well that they sometimes identify false positives or errors that are not actually wrong. It's a sign that they are heavily invested in the work, and I love to see that.

## Change It Up

One great tweak to this type of prompt is to get specific about the number and kind of errors that you want the AI to include:

> ✦ Describe the differences between tap dance and Bollywood dance styles. Include three errors about the type of music for each.

And here is a tip from my own experience: Don't forget to ask the chatbot to tell you which errors it has added:

> ✦ Describe the differences between tap dance and Bollywood dance styles. Include some errors about the type of music for each. Provide an answer key with explanations.

Since it can be tough for students (and sometimes teachers) to recognize the intentional mistakes in the text, I like to have an answer key that I can give to students who just can't seem to find all the errors.

## Try It Yourself

This is a fun one for students, so I strongly recommend giving it a try right now. Capture your thinking in the following space so that you can put this prompt to use with your students in no time.

---

---

---

---

---

---

---

---

---

## Chapter Reflection

Perhaps no other instructional decision is as important as the one that an educator makes after learning the answers to the question, Who gets it and who doesn't? The heart of what teachers do is identifying what a student needs to continue learning. This means seeing learning gaps and helping students close them and finding ways to stretch the mental muscles of those students who have mastered the lessons. It's at this point in the learning cycle that some students will need to be guided back to a new approach to the content and others will need to start a new cycle. No other part of the process of education relies so much on the judgment and experience of a teacher.

In this chapter, we looked at ways to simplify and streamline the creation of remediation resources by starting with brainstorming (Figuring Out How to Help), then created simple explainers and lists of resources (Breaking It Down and Reteaching Them), and explored a variety of different reteaching lesson ideas (Using a Video Better, Listening to Learn, and Letting Them Create). To enhance learning, we discussed the importance of mindfulness (Centering the Mind). For students ready for more, we explored prompts that can create opportunities to go further (Writing to Learn and Beating the Bot) and ways to motivate students with a view of the future (Seeing Where We're Going).

# Chapter 5 Questions for Discussion

How do you feel about your ability to reach students who need reteaching? How have the prompts in this chapter changed your thinking?

How much of your time and energy is spent on enrichment? Have the prompts in this chapter changed your plans for this important element of teaching?

Do you already employ any of the strategies from this chapter? How might AI tools change your use?

# Epilogue

"I'm not coming back after the holiday break."

The words echoed in my head after my close friend and teammate said them to me in the fall of 2022. She had been an amazing classroom teacher for more than ten years—inspiring middle school students to advocate for social change and finding innovative ways to connect with each one. For the five years we had worked together, she was the teacher I tried to emulate in my own classroom. Overwhelmed with the challenges of being a public school teacher, she took a training job in the private sector. I was heartbroken—for my own loss of a colleague and the loss of amazing educational experiences for my students.

Anyone who has worked in a classroom since the COVID-19 pandemic is aware of the ways that our job has become more difficult, from students readjusting to in-person classes to concerns about learning loss and social development. Even as we begin to close the academic gaps, we are seeing more issues—attendance, antisocial behaviors, lack of resilience and grit—bubble to the surface (Polikoff, Rapaport, Saavedra, & Silver, 2023). Educators all over the world can attest to the persistent vacancies that these challenges have brought about. In the United States alone, teacher turnover has reached alarming levels (Lurye & Griesbach, 2022). There are many reasons that teachers choose to leave the classroom—health issues, needing to care for loved ones, concerns about academic freedom, and classroom management challenges, just to name a few. Several studies have found that managing the teaching workload is near the top of the list (Amitai & Van Houtte, 2022; García, Han, & Weiss, 2022).

The departures of burned-out teachers leave behind vacant positions that many schools struggle to fill (Nguyen, Lam, & Bruno, 2022). Left with no other choice, some school leaders are forced to ask other teachers to pick up the slack. This just exacerbates the problem, as it pushes more teachers closer to their limits. If we are to slow the revolving door of teachers on their way out of our schools, could AI be part of the answer? I believe it is.

Artificial intelligence is going to change the face of education. As these LLMs become more powerful, they will be able to create, evaluate, and analyze like never before. They will someday reach a level of complexity at which they will be able to make some decisions as well as a human could. Make no mistake: They will be able to complete *some* of the tasks that we rely on teachers for but never *all* of what we do. It is the nature of technological advancement to take over some of what humans have done in the past, and it is not something that we can stop.

Throughout this book, however, I have made the case for why teachers should spend some of their limited time and energy learning about and embracing AI as a tool. I have shown you what generative artificial intelligence can provide you and your students. I have demonstrated for you how these tools enhance the work that we do by making high-quality instructional strategies (many of which have demonstrated benefits to learning proven over decades) more practical for more teachers to implement. But so much of what I have shared here is changing rapidly as AI companies upgrade their models and the products that they offer based on them, and it can feel like staying up to date is an impossible task. The key, though, is having a handful of reliable sources of news and recommendations that you consult from time to time. Here are some that I would suggest bookmarking or adding to your social media feed.

- **AI for Education (LinkedIn):** www.linkedin.com/company/aiforeducation
- **The Rundown (email newsletter):** www.therundown.ai
- **AI News (EdSurge):** www.edsurge.com/news/topics/artificial-intelligence
- **Google Alert:** Set up a Google Alert with the keywords "AI education"; www.google.com/alerts

I do not believe that AI will ever completely replace classroom teachers because what it does well is only a small piece of what teachers provide to students and communities. Teachers forge relationships that make students feel welcome, safe, and respected. Teachers manage the dozens of personalities and strengths and needs within their classes while seamlessly adjusting their lessons on the fly. Teachers make thousands of tiny decisions every day to find the best path for each student to reach success.

But it's when we combine the savvy decision-making skill of teachers with the endless time and energy of AI technology that we see both achieve their potential. We can imagine better lessons, build more engaging experiences, and achieve more meaningful learning. And we can amplify the power of good teachers when we give them an assistant that can brainstorm hundreds of ideas in a minute and generate pages of customized learning materials in seconds, freeing those teachers to put these resources to work unlocking the potential of every student.

# References and Resources

Agarwal, P. K., D'Antonio, L., Roediger, H. L. III, McDermott, K. B., & McDaniel, M. A. (2014). Classroom-based programs of retrieval practice reduce middle school and high school students' test anxiety. *Journal of Applied Research in Memory and Cognition, 3*(3), 131–139. https://doi.org/10.1016/j.jarmac.2014.07.002

Akinoso, S. O., Agoro, A. A., & Alabi, O. M. (2020). Effect of station rotation mode of instructional delivery for mathematics in the era of advancing technology. *Journal of the International Society for Teacher Education, 24*(2), 60–72.

Ambrose, S. A., Bridges, M. W., DiPietro, M., Lovett, M. C., & Norman, M. K. (2010). *How learning works: Seven research-based principles for smart teaching.* San Francisco: Jossey-Bass.

Amitai, A., & Van Houtte, M. (2022). Being pushed out of the career: Former teachers' reasons for leaving the profession. *Teaching and Teacher Education, 110*, 103540. https://doi.org/10.1016/j.tate.2021.103540

Anders, P. L., & Guzzetti, B. J. (2005). *Literacy instruction in the content areas* (2nd ed.). New York: Routledge. https://doi.org/10.4324/9781003064282

Andrade, H. L. (2019). A critical review of research on student self-assessment. *Frontiers in Education, 4*, 87. https://doi.org/10.3389/feduc.2019.00087

Anonymous (possibly Cheyenne). (ca. 1890). *Ledger book drawing* [Ink, crayon, woven paper]. Brooklyn Museum, New York. Accessed at www.brooklynmuseum.org/opencollection /objects/2123 on June 24, 2024.

Bailey, J. (2024, March 4). *Why AI struggles with basic math (and how that's changing).* Accessed at www.aei.org/technology-and-innovation/why-ai-struggles-with-basic-math-and-how-thats -changing/? on July 26, 2024.

Bailey, K., & Jakicic, C. (2023). *Common formative assessment: A toolkit for Professional Learning Communities at Work* (2nd ed.). Bloomington, IN: Solution Tree Press.

Bell, M. (2020, October 20). *A five-step cycle to improve learning in your classroom.* Accessed at www.routledge.com/blog/article/the-5-steps-of-the-learning-cycle?cmdf=mike+bell+learning+cycle on April 30, 2024.

Bellert, A. (2015). Effective re-teaching. *Australian Journal of Learning Difficulties, 20*(2), 163–183. https://doi.org/10.1080/19404158.2015.1089917

Bent, S. P., McShea, L., & Brennan, S. (2015). The importance of hearing: A review of the literature on hearing loss for older people with learning disabilities. *British Journal of Learning Disabilities, 43*(4), 277–284. https://doi.org/10.1111/bld.12148

Bergman, D., Calzada, L., LaPointe, N., Lee, A., & Sullivan, L. (1998). *Vertical alignment and collaboration.* Accessed at https://files.eric.ed.gov/fulltext/ED421472.pdf on April 30, 2024.

Bernacki, M. L., Greene, M. J., & Lobczowski, N. (2021). A systematic review of research on personalized learning: Personalized by whom, to what, how, and for what purpose(s)? *Educational Psychology Review, 33*(4), 1675–1715.

Berryman, C. K. (1919, October 19). *Long step in the right direction* [Political cartoon]. U.S. National Archives and Records Administration, College Park, MD. Accessed at https://catalog.archives.gov/id/6011588 on June 24, 2024.

Bodner, G. M. (1986). Constructivism: A theory of knowledge. *Journal of Chemical Education, 63*(10), 873.

Boss, S., Larmer, J., & Mergendoller, J. (2013). *PBL for 21st century success: Teaching critical thinking, collaboration, communication, and creativity.* Novato, CA: Buck Institute for Education.

Bostic, J. Q., Nevarez, M. D., Potter, M. P., Prince, J. B., Benningfield, M. M., & Aguirre, B. A. (2015). Being present at school: Implementing mindfulness in schools. *Child and Adolescent Psychiatric Clinics of North America, 24*(2), 245–259. https://doi.org/10.1016/j.chc.2014.11.010

Brewster, C., & Fager, J. (2000, October). *Increasing student engagement and motivation: From time-on-task to homework.* Accessed at https://educationnorthwest.org/sites/default/files/byrequest.pdf on April 30, 2024.

Brophy, J. E. (2004). *Motivating students to learn* (2nd ed.). New York: Routledge.

Brown, T., & Ferriter, W. M. (2021). *You can learn! Building student ownership, motivation, and efficacy with the PLC at Work process.* Bloomington, IN: Solution Tree Press.

Buck Institute for Education. (n.d.). *Gold standard PBL: Essential project design elements.* Accessed at www.pblworks.org/what-is-pbl/gold-standard-project-design on May 6, 2024.

Buzan, T. (2018). *Mind map mastery: The complete guide to learning and using the most powerful thinking tool in the universe.* London: Watkins.

California Department of Education. (2000). *History–social science content standards for California public schools: Kindergarten through grade twelve.* Accessed at www.cde.ca.gov/be/st/ss/documents/histsocscistnd.pdf on May 15, 2024.

Campos, N., Nogal, M., Caliz, C., & Juan, A. A. (2020). Simulation-based education involving online and on-campus models in different European universities. *International Journal of Educational Technology in Higher Education, 17*(1), 8. https://doi.org/10.1186/s41239-020-0181-y

Carpenter, S. K., Pan, S. C., & Butler, A. C. (2022). The science of effective learning with spacing and retrieval practice. *Nature Reviews Psychology, 1*(9), 496–511. https://doi.org/10.1038/s44159-022-00089-1

Casey, M. (2023, May 25). *Large language models: Their history, capabilities and limitations.* Accessed at https://snorkel.ai/large-language-models-llms on July 8, 2024.

Cook, M. P. (2006). Visual representations in science education: The influence of prior knowledge and cognitive load theory on instructional design principles. *Science Education, 90*(6), 1073–1091. https://doi.org/10.1002/sce.20164

Cuban, L. (2004). The open classroom: Were schools without walls just another fad? *Education Next, 4*(2), 68–71.

Czerkawski, B. (2014). Designing deeper learning experiences for online instruction. *Journal of Interactive Online Learning, 13*(2), 29–40.

Dai, F. (2012). English-language creative writing by Chinese university students: The challenges and benefits of creative writing for university students in China. *English Today, 28*(3), 21–26. https://doi.org/10.1017/S0266078412000259

Davies, M. (2011). Concept mapping, mind mapping and argument mapping: What are the differences and do they matter? *Higher Education, 62*, 279–301. https://doi.org/10.1007/s10734-010-9387-6

Deslauriers, L., McCarty, L. S., Miller, K., Callaghan, K., & Kestin, G. (2019). Measuring actual learning versus feeling of learning in response to being actively engaged in the classroom. *Proceedings of the National Academy of Sciences, 116*(39), 19251–19257. https://doi.org/10.1073/pnas.1821936116

Driscoll, M. (2000). *Psychology of learning for instruction* (2nd ed.). Boston: Allyn & Bacon.

Drysdale, J. S., Graham, C. R., Spring, K. J., & Halverson, L. R. (2013). An analysis of research trends in dissertations and theses studying blended learning. *Internet and Higher Education, 17*, 90–100. https://doi.org/10.1016/j.iheduc.2012.11.003

Dweck, C. S. (2006). *Mindset: The new psychology of success.* New York: Random House.

Fagerlie, K. (2023, February 13). *How to master reverse prompt engineering with ChatGPT.* Accessed at www.allabtai.com/how-to-master-reverse-prompt-engineering-with-chatgpt on April 30, 2024.

Federal Communications Commission. (2024, February 27). *E-Rate: Universal service program for schools and libraries.* Accessed at www.fcc.gov/consumers/guides/universal-service-program-schools-and-libraries-e-rate on July 25, 2024.

Feingold, S. (2023, March 8). *What is artificial intelligence—And what is it not?* Accessed at www.weforum.org/agenda/2023/03/what-is-artificial-intelligence-and-what-is-it-not-ai-machine-learning on April 30, 2024.

Ferriter, W. M., & Cancellieri, P. (2017). *Creating a culture of feedback*. Bloomington, IN: Solution Tree Press.

Fitzpatrick, D. (2024, July 10). *3 reasons why teachers like you are turning to Claude AI projects*. Accessed at www.forbes.com/sites/danfitzpatrick/2024/07/10/3-reasons-why-teachers-like -you-are-turning-to-claude-ai-projects on July 20, 2024.

Flaherty, C. (2021, April 5). *What employers want*. Accessed at www.insidehighered.com /news/2021/04/06/aacu-survey-finds-employers-want-candidates-liberal-arts-skills-cite -preparedness on April 30, 2024.

Forsberg, A., Adams, E. J., & Cowan, N. (2021). The role of working memory in long-term learning: Implications for childhood development. In K. D. Federmeier (Ed.), *Psychology of learning and motivation* (Vol. 74, pp. 1–45). Cambridge, MA: Academic Press. https://doi .org/10.1016/bs.plm.2021.02.001

García, E., Han, E., & Weiss, E. (2022). Determinants of teacher attrition: Evidence from district-teacher matched data. *Education Policy Analysis Archives, 30*(25), 1–30. Accessed at https://files.eric.ed.gov/fulltext/EJ1358180.pdf on August 29, 2024.

Goodwin, B., & Rouleau, K. (2022). *The new classroom instruction that works: The best research-based strategies for increasing student achievement*. Arlington, VA: ASCD.

Google. (2024, May 29). *Gemini apps privacy hub*. Accessed at https://support.google.com /gemini/answer/13594961 on June 24, 2024.

Guskey, T. R., & Brookhart, S. M. (Eds.). (2019). *What we know about grading: What works, what doesn't, and what's next*. Arlington, VA: ASCD.

Halverson, E. R., & Sheridan, K. M. (2014). The maker movement in education. *Harvard Educational Review, 84*(4), 495–504. https://doi.org/10.17763/haer.84.4.34j1g68140382063

Hattie, J. (2023). *Visible learning: The sequel—A synthesis of over 2,100 meta-analyses relating to achievement*. New York: Routledge.

Heller, R., & Greenleaf, C. (2007). *Literacy instruction in the content areas: Getting to the core of middle and high school improvement*. Accessed at www.adlit.org/topics/content-area-literacy /literacy-instruction-content-areas-getting-core-middle-and-high-school on April 30, 2024.

Hendry, G. D., Armstrong, S., & Bromberger, N. (2012). Implementing standards-based assessment effectively: Incorporating discussion of exemplars into classroom teaching. *Assessment and Evaluation in Higher Education, 37*(2), 149–161. https://doi.org/10.1080 /02602938.2010.515014

Hulleman, C. S., & Harackiewicz, J. M. (2009). Promoting interest and performance in high school science classes. *Science, 326*(5958), 1410–1412.

Kaiser, N. (2019, May 15). *Challenging misconceptions*. Accessed at https://edu.rsc.org/feature /challenging-misconceptions/3010457.article on April 30, 2024.

Kang, S. H. K. (2016). Spaced repetition promotes efficient and effective learning: Policy implications for instruction. *Policy Insights From the Behavioral and Brain Sciences, 3*(1), 12–19. https://doi.org/10.1177/2372732215624708

Keary, T. (2023, November 21). *AI hallucination*. Accessed at www.techopedia.com/definition /ai-hallucination on April 30, 2024.

Kolb, D. A. (2015). *Experiential learning: Experience as the source of learning and development* (2nd ed.). Upper Saddle River, NJ: Pearson.

Kontra, C., Lyons, D. J., Fischer, S. M., & Beilock, S. L. (2015). Physical experience enhances science learning. *Psychological Science, 26*(6), 737–749. https://doi.org/10.1177/0956797615569355

Låg, T., & Sæle, R. G. (2019). Does the flipped classroom improve student learning and satisfaction? A systematic review and meta-analysis. *AERA Open, 5*(3). https://doi.org/10.1177/2332858419870489

Lage, M. J., Platt, G. J., & Treglia, M. (2000). Inverting the classroom: A gateway to creating an inclusive learning environment. *Journal of Economic Education, 31*(1), 30–43. https://doi.org/10.1080/00220480009596759

Larson, B. E. (2000). Classroom discussion: A method of instruction and a curriculum outcome. *Teaching and Teacher Education,* 16(5–6), 661–677. https://doi.org/10.1016/S0742-051X(00)00013-5

Lee, T. B., & Trott, S. (2023, July 31). *A jargon-free explanation of how AI large language models work.* Accessed at https://arstechnica.com/science/2023/07/a-jargon-free-explanation-of-how-ai-large-language-models-work on April 30, 2024.

Loewenstein, G. (1994). The psychology of curiosity: A review and reinterpretation. *Psychological Bulletin, 116*(1), 75–98. https://doi.org/10.1037/0033-2909.116.1.75

Lurye, S., & Griesbach, R. (2022, September 12). *Teacher shortages are real, but not for the reason you heard.* Accessed at https://news.yahoo.com/teacher-shortages-real-not-reason-120752159.html on April 30, 2024.

Makarevitch, I., Frechette, C., & Wiatros, N. (2015). Authentic research experience and "big data" analysis in the classroom: Maize response to abiotic stress. *CBE—Life Sciences Education, 14*(3). https://doi.org/10.1187/cbe.15-04-0081

Marfilinda, R., Zaturrahmi, & Indrawati, E. S. (2019). Development and application of learning cycle model on science teaching and learning: A literature review. *Journal of Physics: Conference Series, 1317*(1), 012207. https://doi.org/10.1088/1742-6596/1317/1/012207

Marzano, R. J. (2017). *The new art and science of teaching.* Bloomington, IN: Solution Tree Press.

Marzano, R. J., Norford, J. S., & Ruyle, M. (2019). *The new art and science of classroom assessment.* Bloomington, IN: Solution Tree Press.

Marzano, R. J., Pickering, D. J., & Pollock, J. E. (2001). *Classroom instruction that works: Research-based strategies for increasing student achievement.* Arlington, VA: ASCD.

McGarry, K. B. (2016). *An examination of perceived employability skills between employers and college graduates* [Doctoral dissertation, Northeastern University]. Digital Repository Service. http://hdl.handle.net/2047/D20238136

McMillan, J. H., & Hearn, J. (2008). Student self-assessment: The key to stronger student motivation and higher achievement. *Educational Horizons, 87*(1), 40–49. Accessed at www.jstor.org/stable/42923742 on August 29, 2024.

Meer, N. M., & Chapman, A. (2014). Assessment for confidence: Exploring the impact that low-stakes assessment design has on student retention. *International Journal of Management Education, 12*(2), 186–192. https://doi.org/10.1016/j.ijme.2014.01.003

Metz, C. (2023, March 29). *What makes A.I. chatbots go wrong?* Accessed at www.nytimes .com/2023/03/29/technology/ai-chatbots-hallucinations.html on July 26, 2024.

Mirjalili, S. (2023, July 4). *If AI image generators are so smart, why do they struggle to write and count?* Accessed at http://theconversation.com/if-ai-image-generators-are-so-smart-why-do -they-struggle-to-write-and-count-208485 on July 26, 2024.

Moss, C. M., & Brookhart, S. M. (2012). *Learning targets: Helping students aim for understanding in today's lesson.* Arlington, VA: ASCD.

National Governors Association Center for Best Practices & Council of Chief State School Officers. (2010a). *Common Core State Standards for English language arts and literacy in history/social studies, science, and technical subjects.* Washington, DC: Authors. Accessed at www.corestandards.org/assets/CCSSI_ELA%20Standards.pdf on May 15, 2024.

National Governors Association Center for Best Practices & Council of Chief State School Officers. (2010b). *Common Core State Standards for mathematics.* Washington, DC: Authors. Accessed at www.corestandards.org/assets/CCSSI_Math%20Standards.pdf on May 15, 2024.

Nguyen, T. D., Lam, C. B., & Bruno, P. (2022, August). *Is there a national teacher shortage? A systematic examination of reports of teacher shortages in the United States.* Accessed at https:// edworkingpapers.com/ai22-631 on April 30, 2024.

Nordengren, C. (2022). *Step into student goal setting: A path to growth, motivation, and agency.* Thousand Oaks, CA: Sage.

North Carolina Department of Public Instruction. (n.d.). *Standard course of study.* Accessed at www.dpi.nc.gov/districts-schools/classroom-resources/academic-standards/standard-course -study on July 26, 2024.

OpenAI. (2023, November 14). *Privacy policy.* Accessed at https://openai.com/policies/privacy -policy on June 24, 2024.

Page-Voth, V., & Graham, S. (1999). Effects of goal setting and strategy use on the writing performance and self-efficacy of students with writing and learning problems. *Journal of Educational Psychology, 91*(2), 230–240.

Perry, J., Lundie, D., & Golder, G. (2019). Metacognition in schools: What does the literature suggest about the effectiveness of teaching metacognition in schools? *Educational Review, 71*(4), 483–500. https://doi.org/10.1080/00131911.2018.1441127

Polikoff, M., Rapaport, A., Saavedra, A., & Silver, D. (2023). *The kids are all right? What parents really think about how COVID affected children.* Accessed at https://bit.ly/4adjZDH on July 20, 2024.

Poth, R. D. (2023, July 28). *Building your professional learning network.* Accessed at www .edutopia.org/article/professional-learning-networks-teachers on May 6, 2024.

Reis, S. M., & Renzulli, J. S. (2010). Is there still a need for gifted education? An examination of current research. *Learning and Individual Differences, 20*(4), 308–317.

Revelle, K. Z., Wise, C. N., Duke, N. K., & Halvorsen, A.-L. (2020). Realizing the promise of project-based learning. *Reading Teacher, 73*(6), 697–710. https://doi.org/10.1002/trtr.1874

Ritchhart, R., Church, M., & Morrison, K. (2011). *Making thinking visible: How to promote engagement, understanding, and independence for all learners.* San Francisco: Jossey-Bass.

Rudra, S. (2023, March 30). *ChatGPT in education: The pros, cons and unknowns of generative AI*. Accessed at https://edtechmagazine.com/k12/article/2023/03/chatgpt-in-education -generative-ai-perfcon on April 30, 2024.

Sackstein, S. (2017). *Peer feedback in the classroom: Empowering students to be the experts*. Arlington, VA: ASCD.

Sana, F., & Yan, V. X. (2022). Interleaving retrieval practice promotes science learning. *Psychological Science, 33*(5), 782–788. https://doi.org/10.1177/09567976211057507

SAS Institute. (n.d.). *Artificial intelligence (AI): What it is and why it matters*. Accessed at www .sas.com/en_us/insights/analytics/what-is-artificial-intelligence.html on March 2, 2024.

Schmidt, J. A., Kafkas, S. S., Maier, K. S., Shumow, L., & Kackar-Cam, H. Z. (2019). Why are we learning this? Using mixed methods to understand teachers' relevance statements and how they shape middle school students' perceptions of science utility. *Contemporary Educational Psychology, 57*, 9–31. https://doi.org/10.1016/j.cedpsych.2018.08.005

Schwartz, L. (2019, June 4). *Making learning relevant with case studies*. Accessed at www.edutopia .org/article/making-learning-relevant-case-studies on April 30, 2024.

SciShow Kids. (2021, September 27). *What color are stars? | The science of colors!* [Video file]. Accessed at www.youtube.com/watch?v=O3Y5Ww1IUGU on October 21, 2024.

Sherrington, T., & Caviglioli, O. (2020). *Teaching walkthrus: Visual step-by-step guides to essential teaching techniques*. Melton, United Kingdom: John Catt.

Smyth, P., & Carless, D. (2021). Theorising how teachers manage the use of exemplars: Towards mediated learning from exemplars. *Assessment and Evaluation in Higher Education, 46*(3), 393–406. https://doi.org/10.1080/02602938.2020.1781785

Sousa, D. A. (2024). *Engaging the rewired brain* (2nd ed.). Thousand Oaks, CA: Corwin Press.

St. Aubin, C. (2023, June 15). *Audio and podcasting fact sheet*. Accessed at www.pewresearch.org /journalism/fact-sheet/audio-and-podcasting on April 30, 2024.

Stallings-Roberts, V. (1992). Subjective grading. *Mathematics Teacher, 85*(8), 677–679. https:// doi.org/10.5951/MT.85.8.0677

Stiggins, R., & DuFour, R. (2009). Maximizing the power of formative assessments. *Phi Delta Kappan, 90*(9), 640–644. https://doi.org/10.1177/003172170909000907

Tegmark, M. (2018). *Life 3.0: Being human in the age of artificial intelligence*. New York: Penguin Random House.

Thompson, C. P., & Hughes, M. A. (2023). The effectiveness of spaced learning, interleaving, and retrieval practice in radiology education: A systematic review. *Journal of the American College of Radiology, 20*(11), 1092–1101. https://doi.org/10.1016/j.jacr.2023.08.028

Tippett, C. D. (2016). What recent research on diagrams suggests about learning *with* rather than learning *from* visual representations in science. *International Journal of Science Education, 38*(5), 725–746. https://doi.org/10.1080/09500693.2016.1158435

Tomlinson, C. A. (2017). *How to differentiate instruction in academically diverse classrooms* (3rd ed.). Arlington, VA: ASCD.

Tomlinson, C. A., Brighton, C., Hertberg, H., Callahan, C. M., Moon, T. R., Brimijoin, K., et al. (2003). Differentiating instruction in response to student readiness, interest, and learning profile in academically diverse classrooms: A review of literature. *Journal for the Education of the Gifted*, *27*(2–3), 119–145. https://doi.org/10.1177/016235320302700203

Tucker, C. (2021, October 29). *The station rotation model: Prioritize differentiation, student agency & 4Cs of 21st-century learning*. Accessed at https://catlintucker.com/2021/10/station-rotation-model on July 26, 2024.

Tyack, D. B. (1974). *The one best system: A history of American urban education*. Cambridge, MA: Harvard University Press.

Vandas, K., Westfall, J., & Duvall, A. (2023). *Learner agency: A field guide for taking flight*. San Diego, CA: Mimi & Todd Press.

Wiliam, D. (2018). *Embedded formative assessment* (2nd ed.). Bloomington, IN: Solution Tree Press.

Wormeli, R. (2024). *Fair isn't always equal: Assessment and grading in the differentiated classroom* (2nd ed.). New York: Routledge.

# Index

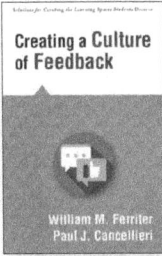

### Creating a Culture of Feedback
*William M. Ferriter and Paul J. Cancellieri*
Because of the importance placed on high-stakes evaluations, schools have built up cultures that greatly emphasize grading. Discover how to shift your classroom focus to prioritize effective feedback over grades, giving students all the information they need to succeed.
**BKF731**

### Making the Move With Ed Tech
*Troy Hicks, Jennifer Parker, and Kate Grunow*
In this book, the authors help educators wade through ed-tech jargon and frameworks to learn how to employ technology tools strategically. Explore moves, or instructional strategies, both familiar and new, that facilitate student inquiry, dialogue, critical thinking, and creativity.
**BKG101**

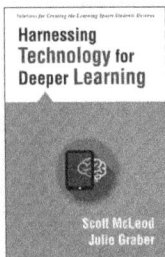

### Harnessing Technology for Deeper Learning
*Scott McLeod and Julie Graber*
Reshape technology integration in classrooms to build truly transformative learning spaces. This reader-friendly guide outlines a clear approach for properly and skillfully using digital tools to promote deeper, personalized learning across subjects and grade levels.
**BKF728**

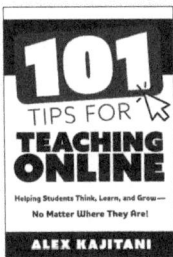

### 101 Tips for Teaching Online
*Alex Kajitani*
Evolve your craft while staying grounded in best teaching practices. Alex Kajitani offers readers a meaningful resource packed with practical tips for making the most of an online classroom community and ensuring your students feel welcomed, engaged, and empowered.
**BKG052**

**Solution Tree | Press** *a division of* Solution Tree

Visit SolutionTree.com or call 800.733.6786 to order.